USDA United States
Department of
Agriculture

Forest
Service

North Central
Research Station

General Technical
Report NC-256

Sampling Protocol, Estimation, and Analysis Procedures for the Down Woody Materials Indicator of the FIA Progam

I0439822

Christopher Woodall and Michael S. Williams

Abstract

The Forest Inventory and Analysis (FIA) program of the USDA Forest Service conducts a national inventory of forests of the United States. A subset of FIA permanent inventory plots are sampled every year for numerous indicators of forest health ranging from soils to understory vegetation. Down woody material (DWM) is an FIA indicator that provides estimates of forest structural diversity, forest area fuel loadings, and national carbon sources. DWM comprises fine woody debris, coarse woody debris, slash piles, duff, litter, and shrub/herbs. Components of DWM are sampled using the line-intersect method and fixed-radius sampling. DWM data analyses serve as integral parts of national inventory reporting requirements, regional/national forest health reports, wildlife habitat assessments, and fuel loading maps. The DWM inventory began in 2001 and is currently implemented in 38 States.

The goal of this document is to provide the rationale and context for a national inventory of down woody material; document the various woody material components sampled by the DWM indicator, the sampling protocol used to measure the DWM components, and estimation procedures; and provide guidance on managing and processing DWM data and incorporating that data into pertinent inventory analyses and research projects.

Cover photos (clockwise): Burnt ponderosa pine log near Prescott, AZ; snail on coarse woody debris in Great Smoky Mountains, NC; fine woody debris near Salinas, CA; and riparian coarse woody debris in Pisgah National Forest, NC.

ERRATA   ERRATA   ERRATA   ERRATA   ERRATA

Please note the following changes to the publication:

Woodall, C.W.; Williams, M.S. 2005. Sampling protocol, estimation, and analysis procedures for down woody materials indicator of the FIA program. Gen. Tech. Rep. NC-256. St. Paul, MN: U.S. Department of Agriculture, Forest Service, North Central Research Station. 47 p.

Overview:

This General Technical Report (GTR-NC-256) broadly describes the down woody materials inventory of the Forest Inventory and Analysis program of the USDA Forest Service. In addition to describing the inventory, it lists estimation procedures/formulae. Some of these formulae have been found to be in error. Based on user/reader feedback, the following notes both correct and clarify some of the formulae in this report. A full revision of the report is currently underway to produce a new edition that follows the structure of inventory estimation procedures documented in SRS-GTR-80 (see Note 11 below for citation) and currently used in national estimation procedures. The revision will be published as a Northern Research Station publication.

Note 1: Formula 3.1, page 16.

$$y = \frac{kac}{L} \sum_{i=1}^{n} d_i^2$$

where y is the volume per unit area, k is a constant that accounts for unit conversions (table 3.1), a is the nonhorizontal lean angle correction factor for the piece of FWD, c is the slope correction factor, L is the total length of transect, d_i is the diameter of the FWD piece at the point of intersection, and n is the number of pieces intersected by the transect. In table 3.1 use only volume constants (V).

Note 2: Formula 3.2, page 16.

$$y^{(w)} = Gy = \frac{Gkac}{L} \sum_{i=1}^{n} d_i^2$$

where $y^{(w)}$ is the FWD dry weight per unit area, G is the specific gravity of the FWD piece. In table 3.1 use only weight constants (W) for k.

Note 3: Formula 3.5, page 18.

$$y = \frac{kc}{L} \sum d_i^2$$

where y is the volume per unit area, d_i is the diameter of the CWD piece at the point of intersection. In table 3.1 use only volume constants (V) for k. If you desire a weight estimate, then use weight constants for k in table 3.1 and G (specific gravity) in the numerator.

Note 4: Formula 3.6, page 18.

$$Var(\bar{y}) = \frac{\pi f}{2AL} \sum_{i=1}^{N} \frac{y_i^2}{l_i}$$

where N is the total number of pieces in the population and A is the area of the study region (DeVries 1986, page 252).

Note 5: Formula 3.7, page 18.

$$Var(\bar{y}) = \left(\frac{\pi f}{2L}\right)^2 \sum_{i=1}^{n} \left(\frac{y_i}{l_i}\right)^2$$

Note 6: Formula 3.11, page 19.

Integrated fuel depth = $\sum_{i=1}^{n} h_i c_i \Big/ \sum_{i=1}^{n} c_i$

Warning: Although the estimator provided in the original publication may provide an adequate estimate of integrated fuelbed depth in some fuel arrangements, it will not accurately reflect the fuel complex in many situations across the United States. To date, no estimator has been forwarded that can adequately estimate the fuel complex in the diverse forest ecosystems of the US.

Note 7: Table 3.4, Volume equations for shape code 3, replaces 3[b] and 3[c] equations

$$V = \frac{1}{12}\pi l\left(h_1 w_1 + \sqrt{h_1 w_1 h_2 w_2} + h_2 w_2\right)$$

where l, h, and w are residue pile dimension measurements.

Note 8. Formula 3.16, page 20

$$Y_{DLF}(c) = (BD)(k)(\bar{y}(c)) = (BD)(k)\frac{\sum_{i=1}^{n} y_i \delta_i}{n_c}$$

where $Y_{DLF}(c)$ is the weight of the duff, litter or fuelbed layer in condition c, BD

the bulk density, k a unit conversion constant, n_c the number of points falling in condition class c, and $\delta_i = 1$ if the i-th point falls in condition class c and $\delta_i = 0$ otherwise.

Note 9: Formulae 3.18, 3.19, 3.20, pages 21-22.

As currently proposed, these formulae will not be used for national estimation of DWM attributes by the FIA program, although these estimators may be appropriate for other down woody inventories in different situations.

Note 10: Incorrect references to formulae:

Page 18, column 1, text line 16: should be equation 3.1
Page 19, column 1, text line 17: should be equations 3.8 and 3.9.
Page 20, column 1, text line 36: should be equation 3.6
Page 20, column 2, text line 30: should be equation 3.8
Page 37, column 1, text line 9: should be equation 3.15
Page 37, column 2, text line 23: should be equation 3.19
Page 38, column 1, text line 9: should be equation 3.20

Note 11: References, pages 32-33.

Revised: Bechtold, W.A.; Patterson, P.L., eds. 2005.
Forest Inventory and Analysis national sample design and estimation procedures. Gen. Tech. Rep. SRS-80. Knoxville, TN: U.S. Department of Agriculture, Forest Service, Southern Research Station. 106 p.

Revised: Harmon, M.E.; Franklin, J.F.; Swanson, F.J.; et al. 1986.
Ecology of coarse woody debris in temperate ecosystems. Advances in Ecological Research. 15: 133-302.

Removed: Stahl, G.; Ringvall, A.; Fridman, J. 2001.
Assessment of coarse woody debris—a methodological overview. Ecology Bulletin. 49: 57-70.

Revised: Van Wagner, C.E. 1968.
The line intersect method in forest fuel sampling. Forest Science 14: 20-26

Revised: Waddell, K.L. 2002.
Sampling coarse woody debris for multiple attributes in extensive resource inventories. Ecological Indicators. 1: 139-153.

Note 12: Appendix 8.4

Any references to appendix 8.4 including PL-SQL code are incorrect. Appendix 8.4 is strictly for processing constants.

Acknowledgments

The Down Woody Materials indicator began as a joint pilot program by the USDA Forest Service Forest Health and Monitoring and Forest Inventory and Analysis programs in the summers of 1999 and 2000. Rick Busing, K. Rimar, Ken Stolte, T. Stohlgreen, and Karen Waddell implemented this initial work. In 2001, the Forest Inventory and Analysis program began to implement a national DWM indicator program. Karen Waddell served as the first national indicator advisor for DWM through the summer of 2002. It is through the pioneering work of these individuals that the DWM indicator exists today.

The authors would like to thank regional trainers, field crews, QA staff, database programmers, and analysts who collect, manage, and disseminate DWM inventory data and products. Finally, the authors would like to thank the following individuals for being instrumental in the development and documentation of the DWM indicator's sample protocols and estimation procedures: Ken Lautsen, Larry DeBlander, Karen Waddell, Olaf Kuegler, and Vicente Monleon.

Table of Contents

Sampling Protocol, Estimation, and Analysis Procedures for the Down Woody Materials Indicator of the FIA Program

1. INDICATOR OVERVIEW

1.1 FIA Inventory and Forest Health Indicators

Forest ecosystems are more than just assemblages of trees. They are associations of flora (i.e., trees, shrubs, herbs, and mosses), fauna (i.e., mammals, amphibians, and soil microbes), and abiotic entities (i.e., decaying organic material, mineral soils, and water) coexisting in complex unity. In recognition of this fact, the Forest Inventory and Analysis (FIA) program of the USDA Forest Service conducts an inventory of our Nation's forest ecosystems that not only estimates tree components, but also inventories numerous nontimber ecosystem attributes (Gillespie 1999, McRoberts et al. 2004, USDA 1999). Estimating various forest ecosystem attributes, instead of focusing solely on trees, may indicate the status and trends in forest ecosystem health. Nontimber ecosystem attributes estimated by the FIA program are collectively referred to as forest health indicators and currently comprise tree crown conditions, ozone injury, tree damage, lichen communities, down woody materials, vegetation structure and diversity, and soil condition (McRoberts et al. 2004).

The down woody materials (DWM) indicator is sampled in conjunction with FIA's national sampling protocol. Sampling of DWM occurs on a subsample of FIA's regular forest inventory plots. FIA's national sampling protocol, for all phases of inventory excluding forest health indicators, is detailed in Bechtold and Patterson (In press). Briefly, FIA's national program consists of three phases of data collection, although these phases are not equivalent to three-phase sampling (see Cochran 1977, Chapter 12). During the first phase of inventory, auxiliary information is collected to poststratify forest inventory ground plots into a minimum of two strata—forest and nonforest. This stratification of inventory sample plots is used to improve the precision of estimates of population totals.

In phase 2 of the FIA inventory, information is gathered from a network of permanent ground plots, with a spatial sampling intensity of approximately one plot per 6,000 acres. Each FIA phase 2 plot consists of four 24-foot fixed-radius subplots arranged in a clustered formation (fig. 1.1). Additional plots are used in some situations. The third and final phase of the FIA inventory involves the sampling of forest health indicators such as DWM. The DWM sampling protocol is applied to a subset of phase 2 inventory plots

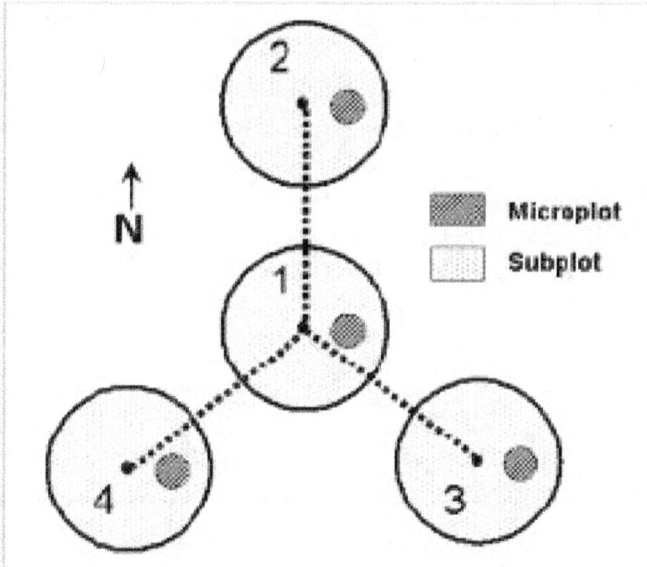

Figure 1.1.—The Forest Inventory and Analysis program's (USDA Forest Service) phase 2 sampling design.

About The Authors:

Christopher Woodall is a Research Forester with the Forest Inventory and Analysis unit at the North Central Research Station in St. Paul, MN. He holds a B.S. in forest resource management from Clemson University and a M.S. and Ph.D. in forest science from the University of Montana. He joined the North Central Research Station in 2001 where his research has focused on individual tree growth/mortality models, fuel dynamics, and innovative forest inventory analysis methodologies. He has served as the national indicator advisor for DWM since 2002.

Michael S. Williams is a mathematical statistician with the Forest Inventory and Analysis unit in Ft. Collins, CO. He holds a M.S. in math, M.S. in statistics, and is currently working on a Ph.D. in forestry at Colorado State University). His most recent research interests include the development of new sampling strategies for standing and downed woody materials, the integration of remotely sensed and ground data, comparisons between design- and model-based inference and the impacts of model failure, and the development of efficient sampling designs for the concurrent estimation of both sample survey and spatial estimation problems.

(approximately 1/16 of all phase 2 plots). The National Sample Design and Estimation Procedures manual details the first two phases of the FIA sampling protocol (Bechtold and Patterson, In press); separate sample design documents for each indicator collectively describe the third inventory phase. This document details the sampling protocol and estimation procedures for the DWM indicator in context of FIA's national sampling protocol.

1.2 The Down Woody Materials Indicator

The DWM indicator estimates dead organic materials (resulting from plant mortality and leaf turnover) and fuel complexes of live shrubs and herbs. Specifically, components estimated by the DWM indicator are fine woody debris, coarse woody debris, litter, duff, fuelbed, slash piles, live/dead shrubs, and live/dead herbs. Definitions, sample designs, and estimation procedures for each DWM component will be described in subsequent chapters.

1.2.1 DWM as it Relates to Fire, Wildlife, and Carbon Modeling Sciences

Scientists from many disciplines may use DWM data to quantify numerous aspects of forest ecosystems. These scientists include but are not limited to wildlife biologists, ecologists, fuels specialists, foresters, carbon/climate change modelers, and criterion/indicator analysts. The DWM indicator, coupled with the entire integrated FIA program, can provide information on the fuels, carbon pools, and wildlife habitat of our Nation's forest ecosystems to policy-makers, scientists, States, and concerned citizens as a whole.

The fine and coarse woody components of the DWM indicator were specifically designed to match the components defined by the National Fire Danger Rating System (NFDRS). This system divides fine and coarse woody debris into size classes that are equivalent to the fuel-hour class system (1-hour, 10-hour, and 100-hour) used by many fire scientists (table 1.1) (Burgan 1988, Deeming et al. 1978). Additionally, numerous other components of the DWM indicator may aid the fire sciences. Litter and duff depths are sampled for estimates of fuel loadings, while estimates of fuelbed depths and microplot vegetative structures (both dead and living) can provide estimates of the spatial aspects of forest fuel complexes. Coupled with the entire FIA inventory, the DWM inventory can be used to estimate fuel loads at strategic scales across the United States.

The United States, mirroring efforts by other countries (Woldendorp et al. 2002), is attempting to quantify forest ecosystem carbon pools (criterion 5, criteria and indicators for the conservation and sustainable management of temperate and boreal forest) (Anonymous 1995, 1997; McRoberts et al. 2004). This quantification of the carbon budget can aid efforts to better understand climate change and the role of forest carbon dynamics in climate change scenarios. The DWM indicator may help in increasing the precision of carbon pool estimates across the United States. Estimates of DWM components, such as coarse and fine woody debris, may be coupled with phase 3 estimates of soil organic carbon content and phase 2 estimates of tree carbon to create comprehensive forest ecosystem carbon estimates (O'Neill et al. 2004, 2005). The FIA program, with all phases contributing toward a comprehensive assessment of total forest carbon, is the only national public database that can estimate and provide continuous monitoring of forest carbon pools in the U.S. (Heath and Birdsey 1997).

Table 1.1.—Fuel-hour and FIA fine/coarse woody debris diameter classes

Transect diameter (in.)	DWM class name	Fuel-hour class (hr)
0.00-0.24	Small FWD	1
0.25-0.99	Medium FWD	10
1.00-2.99	Large FWD	100
3.00+	CWD	1,000+

DWM components, such as coarse woody debris, serve as critical habitat for numerous flora and fauna. From "nurse logs" in the Pacific Northwest to black bear dens in the Southeast, many species find their ecological niche in the shelter that DWM provides. Flora use the microclimate of moisture, shade, and nutrients provided by CWD to establish regeneration (Harmon et al. 1986). CWD provides a diversity (stages of decay, size classes, and species) of habitat for fauna (ranging from large mammals to invertebrates) (Bull et al. 1997, Harmon et al. 1986, Maser et al. 1979). Due to the possibility of dwindling habitat for many native species across our Nation, inventories of DWM are important for habitat assessments and wildlife conservation efforts.

1.2.2 Detection and Evaluation Monitoring

Besides providing estimates and associated variances for various DWM components at various spatial scales, the DWM indicator serves in the broader context as a monitoring tool of forest ecosystem health. Data from other phases and forest health indicators of the FIA program have been used to evaluate the status, changes, and trends in forest health conditions on an annual basis across all ownerships (Keyes et al. 2003). Forest heath monitoring typically involves detection, evaluation, and intensive site monitoring (Keyes et al. 2003). The baseline down woody inventory, provided by the DWM indicator, may be used to detect regional disparities in wildlife habitats or prominent fire hazards. Once possible forest health hazards are detected, these areas may be further evaluated with additional phase 3 plots (plot intensification) or through the implementation of additional studies (intensive site monitoring) (Tkacz 2002). For example, through analysis of baseline DWM inventory for Minnesota, it may be observed that fuel loadings for the Boundary Waters Canoe Area are abnormally high (e.g., fig. 5.4). Because this may be a forest health hazard, phase 3 plots may be intensified to refine both loading estimates and mapping efforts. Therefore, the DWM indicator serves as a baseline inventory for detecting and evaluating forest health hazards.

1.2.3 Current and Expected Outputs

DWM plays a varied role in many ecosystem processes. As such, the data analysis techniques vary depending on the specific issue being addressed. The DWM inventory may be used to address three primary issues:

- Classification of individual plots into various categories. Reasons for classifying individual plots can be quite varied. For example, an analyst might want to determine whether the amount of CWD on a plot meets the requirements for suitable habitat or an analyst may want to search for relationships between the shrub/forb fuel ladders and the overstory of the plot.
- Estimation of per/acre or per/hectare values for plots. These values may be mapped to determine spatial patterns in DWM or monitored over time to indicate changes in the DWM resource.
- Estimation of population totals, which could be used for assessments of the amount of carbon sequestered in DWM.

Estimation techniques for classifying plots and estimating population totals are identical in many cases. However, the techniques differ when specific subpopulations are estimated. FIA recognizes two different types of subpopulations: membership in a subpopulation is determined by either characteristics of individual pieces of DWM or characteristics of the land on which the DWM is located. The term *domain* is used to refer to subpopulations determined by the status of individual pieces of DWM (e.g., species, decay status, fuel class). The term *condition class* is used to denote area-based subpopulations, which can be mapped on the ground (e.g., forest type, ownership).

Current outputs from the DWM indicator can be broadly grouped into the following categories: raw field data, core tables, tabular/graphical summarizations of core tables, and maps. Raw field data are organized into tables according to the DWM component (e.g., fine or coarse woody debris) and the sampling protocol that facilitates its estimation. The six tables containing the DWM field data are coarse woody debris (table 1.2), fine woody debris (table 1.3), fuelbed (table 1.4), transect (table 1.5), piles (table 1.6), and shrub/herbs (table 1.7).

Table 1.2.—Coarse woody debris field data

Plot	Sub-plot	Tran.	CWD dist.	Spp	Tran dia.	Small dia.	Large dia.	Length	Decay class	Hollow	CWD hist.
xxxx	x	xxx	xxx.y (ft)	xxx	xxx (in.)	xxx (in.)	xxx (in.)	xxx (ft)	x	x	x
1	1	030	3.5	317	3	3	5	6	2	N	1
1	1	030	4.0	316	11	5	12	22	3	N	1
1	2	030	22.7	316	7	5	8	19	4	N	1
1	3	150	11.1	317	5	4	5	12	1	N	1
1	3	150	2.2	802	9	7	11	37	3	N	1
1	3	270	7.0	316	5	5	6	28	5	N	1
1	3	270	15.6	802	3	3	4	24	2	N	1
1	4	270	21.0	802	17	15	18	57	3	Y	1
1	4	270	2.9	202	7	5	7	42	2	N	1
2	1	30	17.1	317	14	13	18	40	2	N	1
2	2	30	19.9	317	12	10	15	35	1	N	1
2	2	150	10.3	802	8	7	9	6	3	Y	1
2	2	270	8.7	317	5	4	6	7	2	N	1
2	3	270	3.1	316	8	5	9	31	2	N	1
2	3	270	11.0	316	7	4	11	29	2	Y	1
2	4	30	7.5	317	5	4	9	31	2	Y	1
2	4	150	17.1	317	7	4	9	31	2	Y	1
2	4	270	16.4	316	6	4	10	32	3	N	1

Table 1.3.—Fine woody debris field data

Plot	Sub-plot	Cond. class	Small FWD	Medium FWD	Large FWD	Reason high	Residue pile
xxxx	x	x	xxx	xxx	xxx	x	x
1	1	1	0	0	2	0	0
1	2	1	8	6	3	0	0
1	3	1	3	1	1	0	0
1	4	1	0	3	1	0	0
2	1	1	5	4	1	0	0
2	2	1	1	1	2	0	0
2	3	1	0	2	1	0	0
2	4	2	0	1	4	0	0
3	1	1	6	2	1	0	0

Table 1.4.—Fuelbed field data

Plot	Sub- plot	Transect	Sample taken	Duff depth	Litter depth	Fuelbed depth
xxxx	x	xxx	x	xx.y (in.)	xx.y (in.)	xx.y (ft)
1	1	30	Y	0.2	0.9	2.2
1	1	150	Y	0.8	1.9	4.5
1	1	270	N	0	0	0
1	2	30	Y	0.2	2.0	1.9
1	2	150	Y	1.1	1.7	1.0
1	2	270	Y	0.5	0.8	0.5
1	3	30	Y	0.6	1.9	2.0
1	3	150	Y	0.5	3.2	1.9
1	3	270	Y	0.9	3.0	1.7

Table 1.5.—Transect field data

Plot	Subplot	Transect	Cond. class	Begin slope dist1	Slope pct	End slope dist2
xxxx	x	xxx	x	xxx.y (ft)	xxx (%)	xxx.y (ft)
1	1	30	1	0.0	10	24.0
1	1	150	1	0.0	5	24.0
1	1	270	1	0.0	6	24.0
1	2	30	1	0.0	7	24.0
1	2	150	1	0.0	2	24.0
1	2	270	1	0.0	3	24.0
1	3	30	2	0.0	5	24.0
1	3	150	2	0.0	4	24.0
1	3	270	2	0.0	5	11.5
1	3	270	1	11.6	2	24.0
1	4	30	1	0.0	4	24.0
1	4	150	1	0.0	3	24.0
1	4	270	1	0.0	5	20.5
1	4	270	3	20.6	2	24.0
2	1	30	1	0.0	3	24.0
2	1	150	1	0.0	2	24.0
2	1	270	1	0.0	2	24.0
2	2	30	1	0.0	4	24.0
2	2	150	1	0.0	0	24.0
2	2	270	1	0.0	2	24.0
2	3	30	9	0.0	0	24.0
2	3	150	9	0.0	0	24.0
2	3	270	9	0.0	1	2.1
2	3	270	1	2.2	3	24.0
2	4	30	1	0.0	2	24.0
2	4	150	1	0.0	2	24.0
2	4	270	1	0.0	3	24.0

Table 1.6.—*Slash pile field data*

Plot	Sub-plot	Cond. class	AZ	Shape	L1	L2	W1	W2	HT1	HT2	Density
xxxx	x	x	xxx (°)	x	xx (ft)	xx (ft)	xx (ft)	xx (ft)	xx (ft)	xx (ft)	xx (%)
1	1	1	140	4	10	9	4				10
2	3	1	285	3	15	7	5				20
5	1	1	39	2	22	11	6				20
9	2	1	177	3	7	15	4				30
15	3	1	112	1	16	14	9				10
27	3	2	127	2	10	7	11				20
35	4	1	50	3	14	9	10				20
45	1	1	15	3	20	11	9				30
46	3	3	30	2	21	14	8				10

Table 1.7.—*Microplot fuel loading field data*

Plot	Sub-plot	Live shrub cover	Live shrub HT	Dead shrub cover	Dead shrub HT	Live herb cover	Live herb HT	Dead herb cover	Dead herb HT	Litter cover
xxxx	x	xx (%)	xx.y (ft)	xx (%)	xx.y (ft)	xx (%)	xx.y (ft)	xx (%)	xx.y (ft)	xx (%)
1	1	30	6.1	0	0.0	60	1.2	1	1.2	60
1	2	60	5.7	0	0.0	30	1.9	0	0.0	30
1	3	40	4.0	1	3.1	20	1.5	0	0.0	80
1	4	0	6.3	0	0.0	1	2.0	0	0.0	100
2	1	70	5.3	10	4.6	0	1.5	0	0.0	90
2	2	90	4.1	0	0.0	60	1.6	5	2.2	85
2	3	10	5.0	1	0.7	0	1.5	1	1.8	95
2	4	50	7.8	20	4.0	10	2.0	0	0.0	82
3	1	60	2.9	0	0.0	20	1.1	0	0.0	90

The FIA program uses the term "core tables" to refer to standard tabular summaries of inventory data. For phase 2 of FIA's inventory core tables may consist of per acre estimates of standing timber volume and number of trees. Core tables for the DWM indicator will consist of processed DWM inventory field data. For example, for one FIA plot there may be a dozen CWD pieces. A database-processing algorithm may estimate a single value of CWD tons/acre for that plot. The resulting output from this and other database-processing algorithms populates core tables. Fuel loading-oriented core tables provide plot-level estimates of forest fuel tonnage (table 1.8), while carbon or wildlife core tables contain processed outputs intended for their respective disciplines.

Tabular and graphical summaries of core tables provide more user-friendly outputs for interpreting DWM estimates. Because the phase 3 inventory uses sampling protocols and sample intensities different from the associated phase 2 inventory, graphing DWM component estimates and associated variances may better facilitate inventory dissemination and interpretation (fig. 1.2). The DWM indicator uses a sampling intensity sufficient to indicate the current status and trends in DWM components across large regions of the U.S., thus table summaries should be at larger scales than typically found in State phase 2 inventory reports (example: see Schmidt et al. 2000).

Table 1.8.—*Processed DWM data oriented toward fuel loading output, plot-level*

State	County	Plot	1-hr*	10-hr*	100-hr*	1,000-hr*	Duff*	Litter*	Herb/shrub (ft)	Total tons*
X	17	385	0.2	0.5	1.9	2.6	5.3	0.7	1.0	11.2
X	31	434	0.4	0.5	0.7	1.0	5.6	1.9	0.3	10.1
X	31	436	0.5	1.1	2.6	5.0	3.5	1.6	1.3	14.3
X	31	439	0.7	1.4	4.1	4.6	9.1	3.3	0.7	23.2
X	31	442	0.1	1.3	2.6	3.0	4.9	2.2	0.5	36.8
X	31	446	1.1	2.6	3.0	5.5	15.6	2.1	5.6	29.9
X	31	109	0.9	1.5	9.3	10.4	3.8	3.3	0.8	29.2
X	31	120	1.3	0.8	5.5	1.8	4.7	1.5	0.4	15.6
X	31	900	0.4	1.4	3.3	3.2	17.8	1.9	2.8	28.0

* Tons/acre

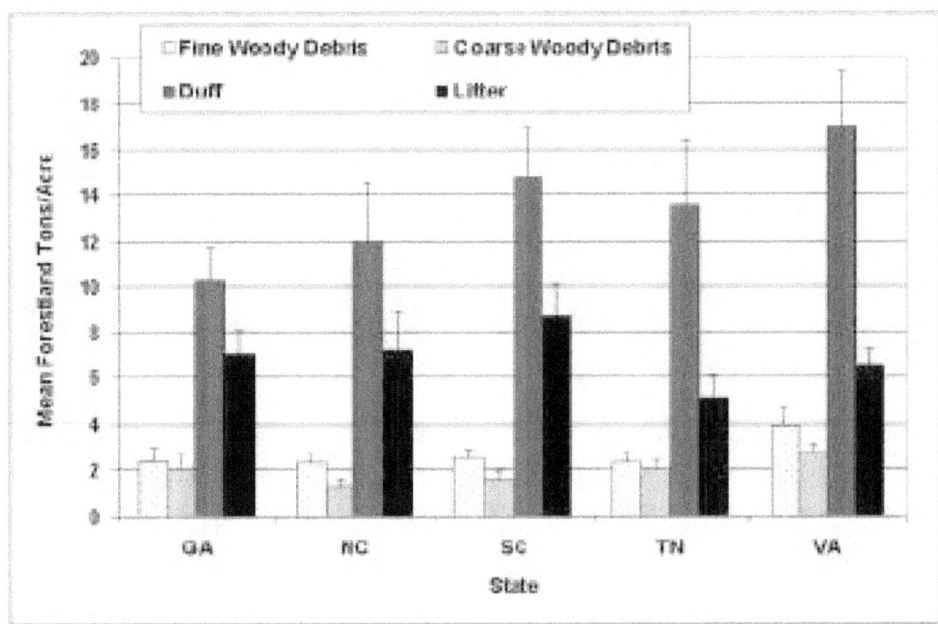

Figure 1.2.—Graphical summary example of processed FIA DWM data for certain States.

Maps of DWM component estimates give analysts the ability to estimate not only the amount, but also the location of DWM components such as duff (fig. 1.3). DWM maps are most successfully created through full analytical integration of all three phases of the FIA inventory. Due to the relative low sample intensity of the DWM indicator, modeling efforts with associated phase 2 plots, along with phase 1 remotely sensed imagery, are often used (Woodall et al. 2004).

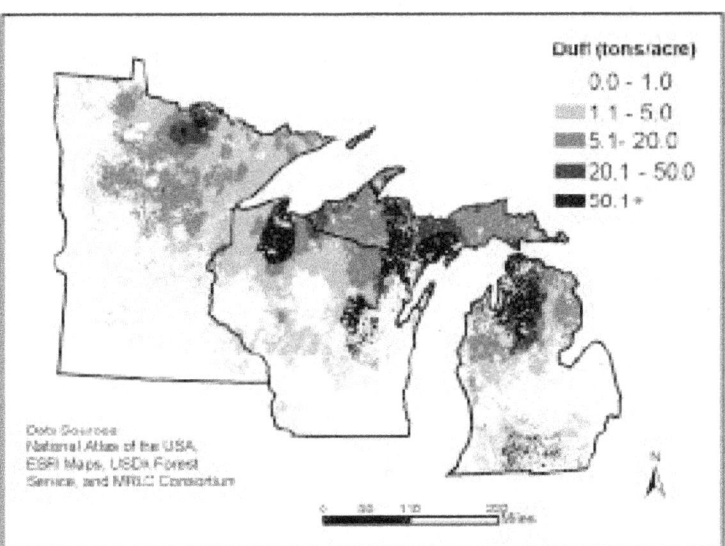

Figure 1.3.—Preliminary map of duff tonnage estimates of North Central States.

Additional outputs of the DWM indicator involve refining many of the current outputs of the DWM indicator. Future work may include development of new mapping methodologies, more sophisticated data processing algorithms, seamless integration with other FIA inventory phases, and integration into State/regional reports. Other outputs will include population estimates such as tons of CWD by forest type/State/region, in addition to mean/acre estimates. Change estimates will not be provided until remeasurement of DWM plots begins in 2006.

2. PLOT-BASED SAMPLING PROTOCOL

2.1 Introduction and Literature Review

Note: DWM sampling protocols described in this manual are for the field protocol used by the FIA program since 2002. For information on historic DWM sample designs used by the Forest Health Monitoring (1999-2000) and the FIA programs (2001), see appendix 8.5 (figure A, B, and C).

The diversity of ecosystem attributes estimated by the DWM indicator requires a variety of sampling techniques (for a full description of field procedures see USDA 2004) (fig. 2.1). Certainly, FIA field crews cannot efficiently count the number of pine needles and down twigs and measure the duff depth across an entire FIA plot. Hence, the DWM sampling protocol is distinctly different from phase 2 sample techniques used to estimate standing tree populations. The plot-based sampling protocol for DWM components includes:

1. line-intersect sampling for fine and coarse woody debris,

2. simple random sampling for duff, litter, and fuelbed depths,

3. fixed-area plot sampling for estimating the coverage and height of shrubs and herbs,

4. shape and packing ratio estimation for slash piles.

Canfield (1941) introduced the concept of line-intersect sampling (LIS) in reference to determining the volume of range vegetation. Warren and Olsen (1964) introduced the first forestry application of the LIS technique in estimation of logging residue in New Zealand. Before LIS was introduced, down woody debris was sampled by a census of all down woody pieces within a defined area or the use of strip samples. Also known as line-intercept and planar intercept sampling with quibbling differences aside (Gregoire and Valentine 2003, Van Wagner 1982a,b), the fundamental concept of LIS is that sampling of down woody debris occurs along transect lines (fig. 2.2). One of the advantages of the LIS technique is that the total volume in a sampled area can be estimated

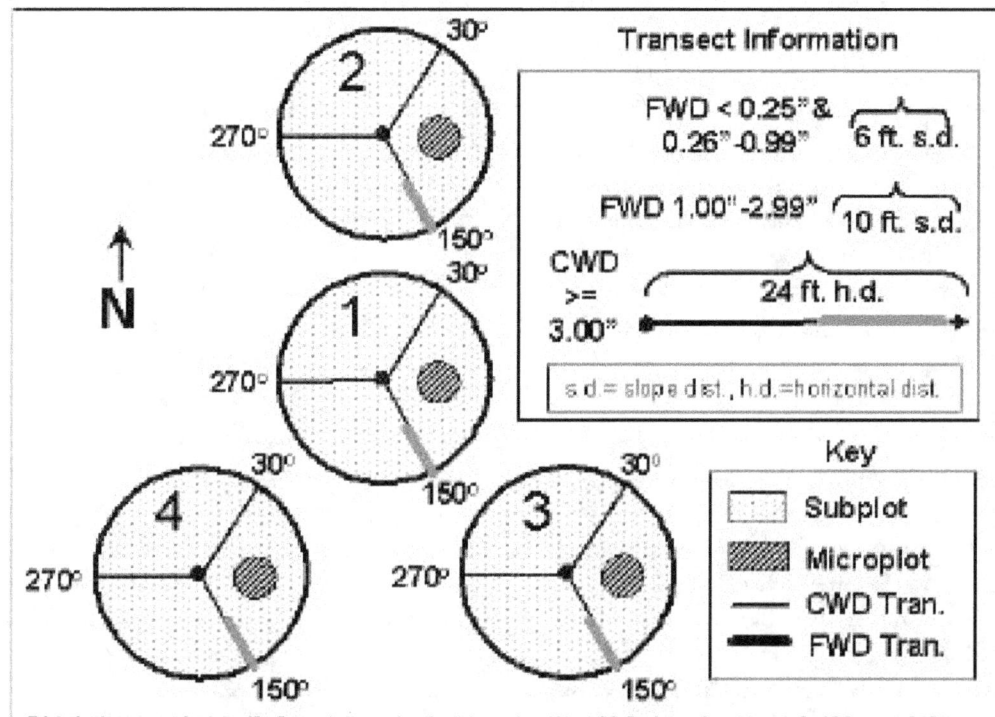

Figure 2.1.—DWM indicator sampling design on an FIA plot (inventory years 2002-present).

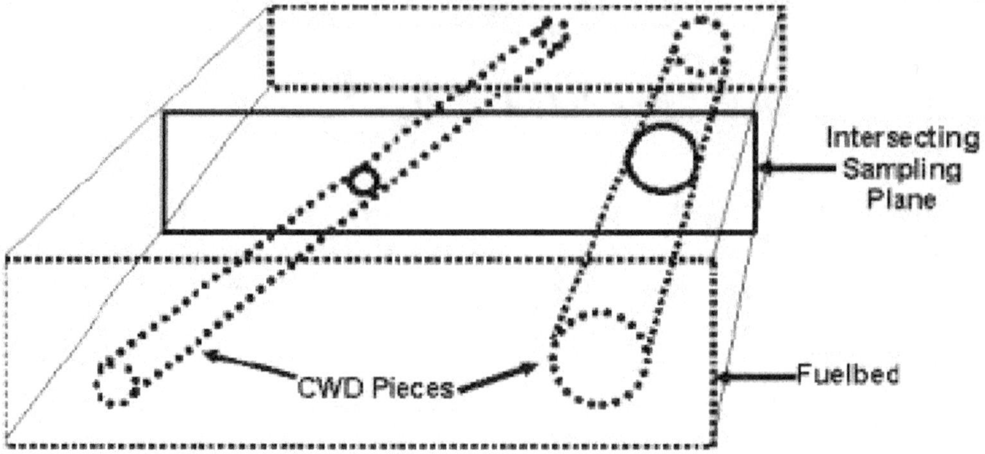

Figure 2.2—Line-intersect sampling planes.

Labels in figure: Intersecting Sampling Plane; CWD Pieces; Fuelbed

by measuring only the diameter or cross-sectional area of a down woody piece at the point of interception by the transect line (Warren and Olsen 1964). Based on this early work, there have been a number of refinements and field applicability alterations for LIS that are reflected in the methods used by the FIA program. Van Wagner (1964) introduced a method for requiring only field measurements of the diameter of each woody piece at transect intersection for determining volume. De Vries (1973, 1974) proposed numerous extensions to the mathematical basis of LIS, and Pickford and Hazard (1978) carried out a series of simulation studies. Brown and Roussopolous (1974) introduced a method for eliminating bias from non-horizontal lean angles of individual woody pieces. Most research of down woody sampling techniques during the 1960s and 1970s was compiled and released in the form of a handbook on inventorying downed woody fuels (Brown 1974). Although restrictive in its array of published estimators and elementary in its methodology, this handbook (Brown 1974) still serves as a key reference for determining fuel loadings across the Western U.S. (Van Wagner 1982a,b).

One point of great confusion regarding LIS is that the properties of the estimators can be derived using both design- and model-based inference. Examples where LIS is derived under the design-based paradigm include Gregoire (1998), Gregoire and Monkevich (1994), Gregoire and Valentine (2003), Kaiser (1983), and Williams and Gove (2003). Examples where model-based inference is used include Bell et al. (1996), Brown (1974), De Vries

(1973), Van Wagner (1982a,b), and Warren and Olsen (1964).

With the increased emphasis on the nontimber attributes of coarse woody debris during the past years, there has been an increase in the development of down woody sampling methods. Recent attention has been given to three possible sources of bias of an LIS estimator. The first is orientation bias. This bias applies only to the model-based approach to LIS and is the bias that occurs when the pieces of DWM tend to be oriented in a particular direction (see Bell et al. 1996), which violates the assumption of a completely random orientation of the pieces of CWD. The second is bias associated with sampling along the boundary of the population of interest (see Ducey et al. 2004, Gregoire and Monkevich 1994, Kaiser 1983 for solutions in the context of design-based inference). The final source of bias is in the potential for applying incorrect estimators in situations where L, Y, X, and triangular transect arrangements are used (Gregoire and Valentine 2003, Marshall et al. 2000, and Ringvall and Stahl 1999). There have also been several studies of the spatial arrangement of woody debris transects within a sampled forest area (Bell et al. 1996, Nemec and Davis 2002). Additionally, new methodology has been proposed for rapid, design-unbiased assessment of coarse woody debris volumes (Bebber and Thomas 2003, Gove et al. 1999, Stahl 1998, Williams and Gove 2003). Finally, there has been increased emphasis on using LIS techniques to estimate not only down woody volumes, but also a range of ecosystem attributes (De Vries 1973, 1974; Kaiser 1983; Marshall et al. 2000; Waddell 2002).

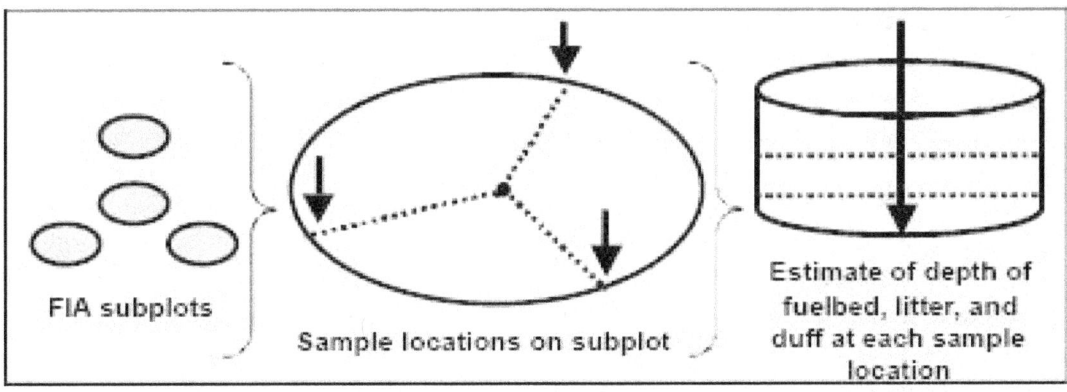

Figure 2.3.—Depth sampling of duff, litter, and fuelbed on an FIA subplot.

FIA subplots

Sample locations on subplot

Estimate of depth of fuelbed, litter, and duff at each sample location

The sampling protocol for the DWM components of litter, duff, and fuelbed involves sampling their depth at various points (point sampling) within FIA subplots (fig. 2.3). Duff, litter, and fuelbed are assumed to be strata of the forest floor such that multiple measurements of their depth may adequately estimate their tonnage and volume (fig. 2.3). Brown (1974) includes simple methodology for recording duff and fuelbed depths that occurs simultaneously as down woody material sampling occurs.

The DWM indicator samples five components on each FIA microplot: dead herbs, live herbs, dead shrubs, live shrubs, and litter coverage (fig. 2.1). Within each microplot, the cover and maximum height of each shrub/herb component is recorded. To produce estimates of tonnage and/or volume of live/dead shrub/herbs, detailed information on species and form must be collected. Because the vegetation structure and diversity indicator collects this information, the DWM indicator does not collect the data necessary for input to shrub/herb prediction equations. However, data from phase 2 and the vegetation indicator (i.e., shrub species and forest type) may be combined with DWM height/coverage data to estimate shrub/herb

volumes/tonnage (Brown and Marsden 1976). Fire scientists may use the height and coverage of shrubs/herbs on the microplot in general assessments of understory fuel ladders (fuel complex). Litter coverage is sampled to estimate the dispersal of litter per unit area of the forest floor. Litter coverage information may augment variance information from the point estimates of litter depth taken on the plot.

The sampling protocol for estimating slash pile volume/tonnage is based on Hardy (1996). We can assume that slash piles are merely conglomerations of woody debris where using transect sampling would be impractical and hazardous. If woody debris is packed into a shape sufficient for ocular delineation, then the dimensions of the shape (fig. 2.4) may be recorded along with an estimate of the packing ratio. The packing ratio, otherwise termed density, is an estimate of the ratio of wood volume to total volume within any defined shape. Bulk density estimates based on the species composition from transect sampled CWD and estimates of packing ratio may be used in slash pile volume equations (Hardy 1996) to provide estimates of tonnage for sampled slash piles.

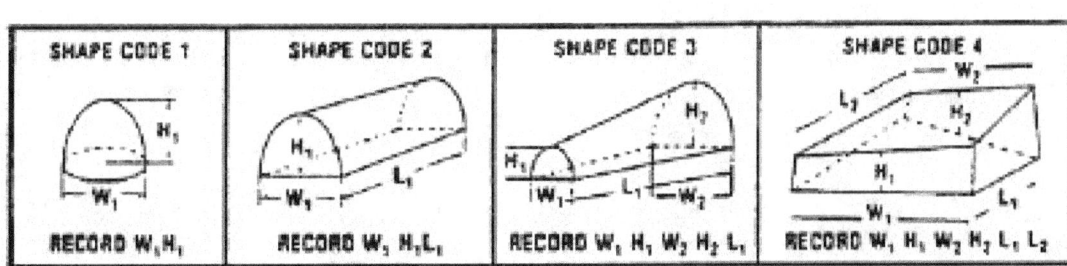

Figure 2.4.—Shape codes for slash piles.

2.2 Fine Woody Debris

The DWM indicator defines fine woody debris (FWD) as down woody pieces with a diameter less than 3 inches at the point of transect intersection. FWD does not include dead branches attached to standing trees, dead foliage, bark fragments, or cubicle rot. FWD is sampled using 6- and 10-foot slope-distance transects co-located on the 150 degree CWD transect on each of the four FIA subplots (fig. 2.1). Three size classes for FWD are related to the hour classes often referenced by fire scientists (table 1.1). Because it would be impractical for field crews to measure the diameter of hundreds of small FWD pieces, field crews estimate tally counts by FWD size class. A 6-foot slope-distance transect is used to tally the smallest class of FWD, while a 10-foot slope-distance transect is used to tally medium and large FWD. The slope (%) of each transect is recorded for use in FWD estimators.

2.3 Coarse Woody Debris

The target population for the DWM indicator is not the population of all fallen dead trees in a forest. Rather, the indicator samples a CWD population of broad interest to numerous FIA customers. Consequently, the DWM indicator defines coarse woody debris (CWD) as downed pieces of wood with a minimum small-end diameter of at least 3 inches and a length of at least 3 feet (for most decay classes). CWD pieces must be detached from a bole and/or not be self-supported by a root system. Additionally, CWD pieces must have a lean angle more than 45 degrees from vertical. The decay class of each CWD piece is rated according to a five-class decay scale (Maser et al. 1979, Sollins 1982) (table 2.1). Decay class information allows determination of tonnage and habitat condition for CWD pieces. CWD pieces classified as most decayed (class 5) must have a length of at least 5 feet. The transect

Table 2.1.—*Decay class information used for rating CWD pieces*

Decay class	Structural integrity	Texture of rotten portions	Color of wood	Invading roots	Branches and twigs
1	Sound, freshly fallen, intact logs	Intact, no rot; conks of stem decay absent	Original color	Absent	If branches are present, fine twigs are still attached and have tight bark
2	Sound	Mostly intact; soft (starting to decay) but can't be pulled apart by hand	Original color	Absent	If branches are present, many fine twigs are gone; those remaining have peeling bark
3	Heartwood sound; piece supports its own weight	Hard, large pieces; sapwood can be pulled apart by hand or sapwood absent	Reddish brown or original color	Sapwood only	Branch stubs will not pull out
4	Heartwood rotten; piece does not support its own weight, but maintains its shape	Soft, small blocky pieces; a metal pin can be pushed into heartwood	Reddish or light brown	Through-out	Branch stubs pull out
5	None, piece no longer maintains its shape, it spread out on the ground	Soft; powdery when dry	Red-brown to dark brown	Through-out	Branch stubs and pitch pockets have usually rotted down

diameter, large-end diameter, small-end diameter, species, decay class, and length are recorded for each CWD piece (except decay class 5).

CWD pieces are selected for sampling based on intersection with any of three 24-foot horizontal distance transects emanating from the center of each FIA subplot (azimuths of 30, 150, and 270 degrees) (fig. 2.1). CWD pieces are tallied with each transect intersection, regardless of the number of intersections. The motivation for using a multi-segmented plot arrangement is to avoid the design bias associated with the failure of the assumption of a nonrandom orientation of pieces of CWD (Bell et al. 1996, Van Wagner 1964). Many authors have voiced concerns about using LIS estimators with transects placed in "Y" arrangements (Gregoire and Valentine 2003, Nemec and Davis 2002, Waddell 2002). In an attempt to address this issue, each arm of the "Y" is treated as an individual transect. There has been some concern about whether the sampling strategy of the "Y" shaped plot and current estimators used by the DWM indicator lead to either a design or model bias (Gregoire and Valentine 2003, Nemec and Davis 2002, Waddell 2002). Simulation studies by Bell et al. (1996) indicate that "Y" arranged CWD transects and their associated estimators have a design bias that is often smaller than would occur if the orientation of the pieces of CWD is not completely random, and a single transect with a fixed orientation is used.

2.4 Duff/Litter/Fuelbed

The DWM indicator defines duff as an organic forest floor layer consisting of decomposing leaves and other organic material. Individual plant parts should not be recognizable in the duff layer. Litter is defined as a forest floor layer of freshly fallen leaves, needles, twigs, cones, bark chunks, dead moss, dead lichens, dead herbaceous stems, and flower parts. The fuelbed is the accumulated mass of all DWM components above the top of the duff layer (excluding live shrubs/herbs). The DWM indicator measures the depth of duff, litter, and fuelbed at 12 locations (24-foot slope-distance on each CWD transect). Measurement errors occur

when crews are not properly trained for identifying the duff layer from mineral soils and the litter layer. Additionally, field crews must be properly trained on how to measure the depth of the fuelbed. Fuelbed measurements are not used to estimate tonnage, but rather to describe the spatial dispersion of fuels from the forest floor up toward the canopy (the fuel complex).

2.5 Shrubs and Herbs

The DWM indicator defines shrubs as herbaceous plants with woody stems. Herbs are defined as nonwoody herbaceous plants, but also include ferns, moss, lichens, sedges, and grasses. Five fuel categories are estimated on each microplot: live shrubs, dead shrubs, live herbs, dead herbs, and litter. The cover from 0 to 100 percent in 10 percent classes is estimated for each of the five fuel categories. The tallest height of all fuel categories (excluding litter) is estimated within the microplot. If available by region, fuel-loading models may use coverage, height, and forest type/understory vegetation information to predict fuel-loading tonnage for microplot fuel categories. Additionally, height and coverage information may be used to estimate the spatial dispersion of microplot fuels similar to the fuelbed measurement.

2.6 Slash Piles

Slash or residue piles are defined as CWD in piles created directly from human activity or from natural events that prohibit safe measurement by CWD transect. If the center of any slash pile coincides with the area sampled by any FIA subplot (24-foot radius) the slash pile is determined as "in." The shape of each tallied slash pile is classified according to a shape code (fig. 2.4) (Hardy 1996). According to the shape code classification, certain dimensions of the pile are measured to the nearest foot. The packing ratio of each pile is estimated. Field crews must be properly trained to ocularly estimate the packing ratio (density) of slash piles. Typically, the packing ratio should not exceed 40 percent.

2.7 Transect Segmenting

To properly attribute estimates of DWM components to appropriate condition classes occurring on any single FIA plot, the condition class along each of the three 24-foot CWD transects is recorded. The condition classes mapped by the DWM indicator match those recorded during phase 2 sampling. This process of recording condition classes along CWD transects is called condition class segmenting. Because CWD, FWD, duff, litter, and fuelbed are measured along CWD transects, the condition class segmenting on these transects is used to facilitate DWM condition class estimation. Additionally, because the microplot is not mapped according to condition class, the condition of the microplot center is thought sufficient for subsequent estimation. The likelihood of the microplot falling on a condition boundary is very small. Thus, any bias associated with the lack of condition class mapping on the microplot is thought to be minimal.

3. ESTIMATION

Producing estimates of DWM components requires coupling appropriate estimators with database programs. Because the users and possible applications of DWM indicator data are so varied, we cannot exhaustively document all possible estimators and database routines here. Instead, a broader view of estimating DWM component values will be presented allowing individual analysts to modify the estimators to suit their needs. Hence, the selection of appropriate estimators depends on the type of analysis being performed. Estimation occurs at three levels: (1) estimating DWM for an individual plot or portion of a plot for classifying the plot (e.g., suitable habitat or fire risk); (2) estimating DWM means for mapping and monitoring; (3) estimating population totals. An important complicating factor is that some plots will cover multiple condition classes. For example, a plot may fall on the boundary between a recent clearcut and a mixed hardwood-softwood stand. In situations such as this, an analyst may want to determine DWM attributes on each of the different condition classes to avoid possible anomalies in the analysis due to the mixing of data from different conditions.

In this section, we begin with the basic methodology for estimation and then provide the estimators used to address the three general types of estimation (i.e., classification, mapping/monitoring, population totals).

3.1 Estimation Methods

3.1.1 The Approach to Inference for Fine and Coarse Woody Debris

Inference for the FWD and CWD is model-based. The assumed model structure for line-intersect sampling is that the location and orientation of the logs within the population is both completely random and independent. These assumptions might not hold in real populations, so the sample design is such that the estimators will be robust to violations of the assumed model. To account for the possibility that the logs are not randomly

oriented, the sampling transects are oriented in multiple directions to reduce an orientation bias (Bell et al. 1999, van Wagner 1968). The sample locations are randomly placed across the populations to account for the concern that pieces of FWD and CWD are not randomly located.

Fewer attributes are estimated for FWD than for CWD. For FWD, only the volume and weight are estimated. Estimating other attributes would require measuring the length of each piece of FWD, which would be impractical and cost-prohibitive for a national inventory program, especially where a large number of pieces of FWD are encountered. For CWD, the volume, weight, number of pieces, suitable habitat, and other attributes can be estimated. Detailed measurements are taken on all pieces of CWD that intersect a transect. The reason for the additional measurements is that habitat assessments often require information that describes the size, shape, and condition of logs to determine if they meet minimum habitat requirements. These habitat assessments are essential for some customer groups. For example, national forests in the Pacific Northwest have adopted guidelines for a minimum retention of CWD. An example given by Marshall et al. (2002) is: "Mixed-conifer stands east of the Cascade Range and the Eastside Forest Plan Amendment stipulate that 15 to 20 pieces per acre, 6 or more feet long, with a total linear length of 100 to 140 feet of pieces 12 inches and greater in a small end diameter."

3.1.1.1 Fine Woody Debris Estimators

De Vries (1986, p. 242-276) provides derivations and discussions of estimators for fine and coarse woody debris sampled by LIS. Many different estimators could be used for estimating FWD, but due to the time-intensive labor required to measure it, only a single estimator is used to estimate FWD volume and weight. The advantage of this estimator is that the length of FWD is not required for estimation. The estimator of volume or weight of FWD for a single transect of length L

for FWD pieces intersected by a transect is as follows:

$$\bar{y} = (kfac)(\pi^2/8L)\sum_{i=1}^{n} d_i^2 \qquad (3.1)$$

where $\bar{y}$ is volume per unit area, k is a constant that accounts for unit conversions (see volume constants, table 3.1), f is a constant for converting the estimates to per acre or per hectare values (see table 3.2), a is the nonhorizontal (lean) angle correction factor for the piece of FWD, c is the slope correction factor, L is the total length of the transect, d_i is the diameter of the piece at the point of intersection, and n is the number of pieces intersected by the transect. The nonhorizontal correction factor, a, may range from 1.00 to 1.40 in value depending on the angle of lean from vertical (0-45 degrees) of each FWD piece (Brown 1974) and is determined by:

$$a = \frac{1}{\cos(h)}. \qquad (3.1a)$$

where a is the nonhorizontal lean angle correction factor and h is the angle of tilt for each FWD piece from horizontal (after Van Wagner 1982a,b).

Because the DWM indicator does not collect the lean angle of individual FWD pieces, analysts must either assume no lean angle or use published lean-angle correction factors for their particular region and/or forest condition.

Additionally, because FIA samples FWD using 6- and 10-foot slope-distance transect lengths, these lengths are corrected for slope using the following equation:

$$c = \sqrt{1 + (\%slope/100)^2}. \qquad (3.1b)$$

where c is the slope correction factor and %slope is the slope percent (Brown 1974).

The weight of FWD is estimated by multiplying the volume by a species- and condition-specific correction factor that accounts for specific gravity. Thus,

$$\bar{y}^{(w)} = G\bar{y} = (Gacfk)(\pi^2/8L)\sum_{i=1}^{n} d_i^2. \qquad (3.2)$$

where $\bar{y}^{(w)}$ is down wood dry weight per unit area. This estimate is derived from the volume estimator, $\bar{y}$, multiplied by G, which is the specific gravity (Brown 1974, Van Wagner 1982a,b) conversion factor (see appendix 8.5).

Both estimators, $\bar{y}$ and $\bar{y}^{(w)}$, are further modified to simplify data collection. Instead of actually measuring the diameter of each piece of FWD, field crews tally the number of pieces of FWD in each of the three FWD size classes (table 1.1). For both equations (3.1 and 3.2), the summation $\sum_{i=1}^{n} d_i^2$ is replaced with $n_s\bar{d}_s^2$, where n_s is the number of pieces of FWD in size-class s and $\bar{d}_s^2$ is the squared mean diameter for pieces within an FWD diameter class. These values might be empirically derived by species because of the differences in

Table 3.1.—Equation (3.1 and 3.2) constants (k) for some length, volume, and weight units (Van Wagner 1982)

	Unit combinations			k
d	L	V	W	
cm	m	m³/m²	-	0.0001234
cm	m	m³/ha	-	1.234
cm	m	-	kg/m²	0.1234
cm	m	-	tons/ha	1.234
in.	ft	ft³/ft²	-	0.008567
in.	ft	ft³/ac	-	373.3
in.	ft	-	lb/ft²	0.5348
in.	ft	-	tons/ac	11.65

branching patterns/sizes and because the distribution of individual FWD sizes within any size class (especially for 1-3 inches) is usually left-skewed. For example, $\bar{d}_i$ of ponderosa pine in the 1- to 3-inch class is 3.12 with a mean diameter of around 1.77 (left-skewed) (Brown 1974). For more common forest types in the Western U.S., there are $\bar{d}_i$ available in the literature. For less common forest types, default values for either conifer or hardwood forest types are used. A partial list is given in appendix 8.4. Many unit combinations and constants may be used in equations 3.1 and 3.2 depending on desired estimates (table 3.1).

3.1.1.2 Coarse Woody Debris Estimators

Numerous model-unbiased estimators exist for assessing CWD when sampling with a single straight-line transect (cf. Brown 1974, De Vries (1986, p. 58, eq. 29, p. 60, eq. 33), Stahl et al. (2001, eqs. 6, 7, 8)). The estimators used with the FIA DWM indicator were chosen for two reasons: (1) to be compatible with existing data, and (2) to have the smallest possible variance. Minimizing the variance of the estimator is an important consideration because line-intersect sampling often requires long transects to achieve high levels of precision (Pickford and Hazard 1978).

In the available literature, De Vries (1986) provides the most complete treatment of line-intersect sampling from the model-based perspective and Brown (1974) provides additional material that is necessary to complete the assessment of CWD. Thus, the results of these two authors will form the basis of the estimation process for CWD.

The formula used for computing an estimate per unit area value when sampling with a single transect of length L is

$$\bar{y} = \frac{f\pi}{2L} \sum_{i=1}^{n} (y_i / l_i) , \qquad (3.3)$$

where $\bar{y}$ is a model-unbiased estimator of the attribute of interest per unit area, f is used to convert the estimate into a per acre or per hectare value, L is total transect length, y_i is the attribute of interest for CWD piece i, and l_i is the length of the piece (see table 3.2).

The need to classify pieces of CWD into specific habitat classes requires additional information on each piece of CWD (e.g., length and small- and large-end diameters). Given these additional measurements, the volume of an individual piece

Table 3.2.—Equations to estimate per unit area values for attributes of individual CWD pieces (De Vries 1986, Waddell 2002)

Attribute	Equation[a]	Units for each equation variable[a]				
		L	V	l	D	f
Cubic feet per ac	$(\pi/2L)(V_A/l)f$	ft	ft^3	ft	in.	43,560 ft^2/ac
Cubic meters per ha	$(\pi/2L)(V_a/l)f$	m	m^3	m	cm	10,000 m^2/ha
Logs per ac	$(\pi/2L)(1/l)f$	ft	-	ft	-	43,560 ft^2/ac
Logs per ha	$(\pi/2L)(1/l)f$	m	-	m	-	10,000 m^2/ha
Tons per ac	$[(\pi/2L)(V_A/l)f][0.0312(G)]$	ft	ft^3	ft	in.	43,560 ft^2/ac
Kg per ha	$[(\pi/2L)(V_a/l)f][1000(G)]$	m	m^3	m	cm	10,000 m^2/ha
Mg of carbon per ha for softwoods	$[(\pi/2L)(V_a/l)f][0.521(G)]$	m	m^3	m	cm	10,000 m^2/ha
Mg of carbon per ha for hardwoods	$[(\pi/2L)(V_a/l)f][0.491(G)]$	m	m^3	m	cm	10,000 m^2/ha

[a] L: total length of the transect line, V_A: volume in cubic feet of individual piece, V_a: volume in cubic meters of an individual piece, l: length of individual CWD piece, f: conversion factor for per acre and per hectare values, G: specific gravity, which will need to be reduced by the necessary decay reduction factor.

can be determined using Smalian's formula (Husch et al. 1972, p. 101)

$$V_{fi} = \frac{(\pi/8)(d_S^2 + d_L^2)l}{144} , \quad (3.4)$$

where V_{fi} is volume in cubic feet; d_s and d_L are the small- and large-end diameters (in.) of the CWD piece, respectively; and l is the CWD piece length in feet.

Because of the advanced decay of logs in decay class 5, only the transect diameter is collected. A different estimator is used for this class because pieces of CWD in decay class 5 are often so inconsistently formed that the volume cannot be reliably determined using Smalian's or other simple formulae. The estimator used for CWD in decay class 5 is

$$\bar{y} = \frac{f\pi^2}{8L} \sum_{i=1}^{n} d_i^2 . \quad (3.5)$$

which is derived from a FWD estimator (equation 3.2).

Volume information used in conjunction with equation 3.2 will reduce the variance of the decay class 5 CWD estimator. Unpublished simulation studies suggest that reductions in the variance rnaging from 3 to 30 percent are not uncommon when comparing equation 3.2 to equation 3.1. The attributes and the appropriate formulae for both English and metric units are listed in table 3.2.

As given by De Vries (1986, p. 252), variance and a sample-based variance estimator for an individual transect is given by:

$$Var(\bar{y}) = \frac{\pi}{2L} \sum_{i=1}^{n} \frac{y_i^2}{l_i} \quad (3.6)$$

and

$$Var(\bar{y}) = (\frac{1}{2l})^2 \sum_{i=1}^{n} (\frac{y_i}{l_i})^2 . \quad (3.7)$$

However, as noted by Lucas and Seber (1977), these estimators are likely to be unreliable, so estimating the variance through replication is preferable. Because CWD piece locations are assumed to be random and independent, which might not accurately reflect actual field conditions in all situations, care should be given when applying these variance estimators.

For a rather expeditious estimation of certain limited attributes of CWD, analysts may prefer Brown's (1974) estimators. Equations 3.1 and 3.2 may be used to estimate the weight and volume of CWD. However, application of Brown's (1974) estimators does not utilize numerous variables collected by the DWM indicator on individual CWD pieces (i.e., CWD piece length, large-end diameter, and small-end diameter) that may be used for habitat classification or more detailed CWD analyses beyond that of volume or weight determinations. Because CWD is sampled using a horizontal transect, the slope correction factor may be set to 1 or removed from the equation. Additionally, because the DWM indicator collects decay class information, G may be reduced to account for decay reductions (DCR) in specific gravity (Waddell 2002) (table 3.3).

Table 3.3.—Decay class reduction factors for CWD by decay class and species group (from Waddell 2002)

Decay class	Species group	
	Softwoods	Hardwoods
1	1.00	1.00
2	0.84	0.78
3	0.71	0.45
4 and 5	0.45	0.42

3.1.2 Duff, Litter, and Fuelbed

We assume that duff, litter, and fuelbed depths are sampled using simple random sampling (SRS), even though the 12 sampling locations are systematically arranged. The estimate of the mean depth, and its associated variance estimator, are given by:

$$\bar{y} = \frac{\sum_{i=1}^{n_f} y_i}{n_f} , \quad (3.8)$$

$$s_y^2 = \frac{\sum_{i=1}^{n_f} y_i^2 - \frac{(\sum_{i=1}^{n_f} y_i)^2}{n_f}}{n_f(n_f - 1)} . \quad (3.9)$$

where $\bar{y}$ is mean depth, s_y^2 is the variance, y_i is the depth at the ith point, and n_f is total number of points falling in the forested condition.

To determine litter and duff weights per area, the estimators of mean depth are multiplied by fixed conversion factors to estimate the number of tons per unit areas from equation 3.8,

$$\overline{Y}_{ts,r} = \bar{y}(BD)(k) , \qquad (3.10)$$

where $\bar{y}$ is the mean depth of duff or litter, BD is bulk density (i.e., weight per unit volume, lbs/ft³, see appendix 8.5 for example of BD values), and k is unit-area conversion values (21.78 for tons/acre with depth in feet) (10,000 for kg/ha with depth in meters).

3.1.3 Shrubs and Herbs

Because shrub and herb attributes are estimated using SRS, mean and variance estimators (equation 3.9 and 3.10) may be applied to determine mean values (i.e., mean maximum live shrub height) per sample unit (condition class or plot level). As an alternative to reporting mean shrub/herb height and coverage, all these measurements may be incorporated into a single measure of the height of this fuel complex known as the integrated fuel depth. Integrated fuel depth scales the maximum height of all shrub/herb components based on its associated coverage and then determines a mean value:

$$\text{Integrated Fuel Depth} = \sum_{i=1}^{n}\{(h_i(c_i/100)\}/\{(\sum_{i=1}^{n}(c_i))/100\} , \quad (3.11)$$

where n is the number of shrub/herb components, h_i is the height of the ith component, and c_i is the coverage of the ith component.

3.1.4 Slash

Slash or residue pile volumes and weights are determined through estimators provided by Hardy (1996). The first step in estimation is to determine the net volume of the slash pile based on the pile's shape and associated sampled dimensions (fig. 2.4) using equations in table 3.4. Estimates of a pile's net

volume may be converted to an estimator of pile weight (y^{pile}) using:

$$\bar{y}^{pile} = Vol(BD)(P)(k) \qquad (3.12)$$

where Vol is the net volume of the pile, BD is bulk density (mass per unit volume, i.e., lbs/ft³), P is the packing ratio or density of the slash pile, and k is a unit conversion constant.

Table 3.4.—*Equations for determining net volume of slash piles based on shape code (Hardy 1996)*

Shape code	Net volume equation[a]
1	$(\pi h w^2/8)(PR)$
2	$(\pi w l h/4)(PR)$
3[b]	$(\pi l_2[h_1^2+h_2^2+(h_1 h_2)]/6)(PR)$
3[c]	$(\pi l_2[w_1^2+w_2^2+(w_1 w_2)]/24)(PR)$
4	$[(l_1+l_2)(w_1+w_2)(h_1+h_2)/8)(PR)$

[a] h_i, l_i, and w_i refer to pile dimensions according to shape code and PR is packing ratio.
[b] equation if using heights.
[c] equation if using widths

A field crew visually determines the location of the center of a slash pile. Subsequently, the pile is considered "in" if the center point of the pile falls within the boundary of one of the four 1/24-acre subplots. An estimator of the pile weight per unit area for the slash piles found on one FIA subplot is

$$\bar{y}^{pile} = \frac{\sum_{i=1}^{n} y_i^{pile}}{a_f} . \qquad (3.13)$$

where a_f is the area of the subplot covering forested land in the appropriate units, and y_i^{pile} is the pile weight of the ith slash pile on the subplot, and n is the number of slash piles on the subplot.

3.2 Estimation for Plot Classification

Most classification schemes apply a label to a plot based on the estimated per acre value found on the plot. One complicating factor is that FIA plots (and forest inventory plots in general) cover neither an acre nor a hectare. An accepted practice for the purpose of classification is to assume that the plot subsamples either the hectare or acre surrounding the subplot center. This assumption will also be extended to plots that straddle multiple condition classes.

3.2.1 FWD and CWD Classification Methods for a Single Plot

When the entire plot falls in a single condition class, there are $k_f = 4$ FWD transects and $k_c = 12$ CWD transects. In this situation, the per acre (hectare) estimators for FWD and CWD are simply the mean of the estimators derived from the individual transect (equations 3.1 and 3.3). For example,

$$\overline{Y}_{CWD} = \frac{1}{k_c} \sum_{j=1}^{k_c} \overline{y}_j .\qquad (3.14)$$

where $\overline{y}_j$ is the estimator of any CWD attribute derived from the jth transect using equation 3.3. In the remainder of the discussion, we will focus on classification issues for CWD because this attribute is generally much more important when classifying the plot for potential habitat.

Estimation for CWD becomes more complicated whenever a plot straddles more than one condition because there are multiple approaches to combining the estimators from the individual transects and because the number of transects and length of each transect in the condition class are not necessarily constant. To address this situation requires some additional notation, so let $L_j(c)$ be the length of the jth transect in condition class c and $k(c)$ be the number of transects that at least partially cover condition class c. Using the result that the variance increases proportionally with the length of the transect (equation 3.5) and the results of De Vries (1986, p. 254), the best linear unbiased estimator is given by:

$$\overline{Y}(c) = \frac{f\pi}{2 \sum_{j=1}^{k(c)} L_j(c)} \sum_{j=1}^{k(c)} \sum_{i=1}^{n_j} \frac{y_{ij}}{l_{ij}} \qquad (3.15)$$

where y_{ij} and l_{ij} are the attribute of interest and length of the piece of CWD, respectively for the ith piece of CWD tallied on the jth transect (for each condition on each individual subplot), and $\overline{Y}(c)$ is the per acre (hectare) estimator for condition class c.

Two points are worth noting. First, a piece of debris may fall across two or more transects. Additionally, a severely bowed CWD piece may intersect the same transect twice. When these situations occur, the piece is tallied once for each transect that it crosses (i.e., $(y_{ij} = y_{i,j})$). Second, caution must be used when classifying plots that straddle multiple condition classes because $\overline{Y}(c)$ for a condition class can be highly variable and produce nonsensical estimates. These situations can occur whenever a large attribute (y_{ij}) is tallied on a very short total transect length (i.e., $\sum_{j=1}^{k(c)} L_j(c)$ is "small"). The other concern is that no pieces of CWD will be tallied on a short section of transect, which will lead to a zero estimate of CWD per acre in areas that may actually have much higher levels. Although situations such as this are generally rare in FIA, these partial plots should be dropped from the analysts and the classification for the plot that represents the majority of the plot should be used. This result is illustrated in the example in appendix 8.3.

3.2.2 Duff, Litter, and Fuelbed Classification Methods for a Single Plot

Estimation of duff, litter, and fuelbed (DLF) for a single plot is given by equation 3.11. The estimator must be modified slightly whenever a plot straddles more than one condition to properly estimate the DLF for each condition. The estimator for a specific condition class c is

$$\overline{Y}_{DLF}(c) = (BD)(k)(\overline{y})(c) = (BD)(k) \frac{\sum_{i=1}^{n_c} y_i \delta_i}{n_c} , \qquad (3.16)$$

where n_c is the number of points falling in condition class c, and $\delta_i = 1$ if the points fall in condition class c, and $\delta_i = 0$, otherwise. If multiple conditions are encountered on a single plot, then one estimate is generated for each condition (i.e., $\overline{Y}_{DLF}(c)$ and $\overline{Y}_{DLF}(c')$ are calculated for conditions c and c', respectively).

3.2.3 Slash Pile Classification Methods for a Single Plot

It will often be useful to classify individual plots based on certain components of the DWM indicator (i.e., CWD, duff, and litter) in an effort to look for linkages between fuel characteristics and other forest conditions. For example, an analyst may want to determine if 1- and 10-hour fuel levels are higher on private or public lands. However, it seems unlikely that any meaningful information can be gleaned from the location and size of slash piles because these piles are infrequently sampled. Therefore, only an estimator of pile weight per unit area is given in this section.

A ratio of means estimator is used to combine the information from each of the four FIA subplots. Thus, the estimator for the weight of slash piles per unit area is

$$\bar{Y}_{pu} = \frac{\sum_{j=1}^{4} \sum_{i=1}^{n_j} y_i^{pu}}{\sum_{j=1}^{4} a_j(f)} . \qquad (3.17)$$

where y_i^{pu} is the weight of the ith pile on the jth subplot, n_j and $a_j(f)$ are the number of slash piles and the area of forest on subplot j, respectively.

3.3 Estimation of Population Totals by Combining Information from Multiple Plot Estimates

As we discussed in section 3.2.1, the per acre estimates for individual condition classes on a single plot can sometimes be very erratic or unrealistic. Although this would appear to pose problems when estimating population totals, it does not because the estimation of population totals uses a fundamentally different approach to combining the data across plots.

A difficult decision for inventories such as FIA is the description of the target population and the selection of an appropriate sample unit (Williams and Eriksson 2002). The target population for the DWM estimators is all downed woody material covering areas that meet the FIA definition of forested land. Due to the low sampling intensity of approximately one plot every 96,000 acres, the analyses for DWM are usually carried out over areas as large or larger than aggregated counties or States. FIA defines forest land area as land that is at least 10 percent stocked by trees of any size, or land

formerly having such tree cover, and not currently developed for a nonforest use. The minimum area and width requirements for classification as forest land are one acre in size and 120 feet wide, respectively. Grazed woodlands, reverting fields and pastures that are not actively maintained, are included if the above criteria are met. For estimating population totals, the sample unit will be treated as a point. One advantage of using this target population and sample unit is that the area of the target population, denoted by A_y, is already estimated by the FIA program using a combination of the phase 1 and 2 data. Another advantage is that the sample sizes in phase 2 are so large that the variance of the estimator, $\hat{A}_y$, is essentially zero for most DWM analyses.

The population-level estimator requires some additional notation. Let M be the number of plots that fall in the target population, let $m = 1,...M$ index the FIA cluster plots, and let k, index the number of transects, microplots, or duff/litter points, with $*$ indicating the type of attribute being estimated (i.e., FWD, CWD, duff, litter, fuelbed, slash pile). For example, k_c is the number of CWD transects that at least partially cover land that meets the definition of forest. Thus, if all M plots completely covered forested land, the estimator would be:

$$\bar{Y} = \frac{1}{M} \sum_{m=1}^{M} \frac{1}{k_f} \sum_{j=1}^{k_i} \frac{\pi}{2L} \sum_{i=1}^{n_i} \frac{y_{ijm}}{l_{ijm}} . \qquad (3.18)$$

where y_{ijm} is the attribute of interest for the ith piece of CWD tallied on the jth transect of the mth cluster plot. However, it is not reasonable to assume that all plots will fall within the boundary of the forest; some plots will likely straddle the forest-nonforest boundary. In estimating population totals, the length of each transect covering the forest, which is denoted $L_j(f)$, is used and the estimator is

$$(3.19)$$

$$\bar{Y}(f) = \frac{1}{M} \sum_{m=1}^{M} \bar{Y}_m = \frac{1}{M} \sum_{m=1}^{M} \frac{\pi}{2 \sum_{j=1}^{k(f)} L_j(f)} \sum_{j=1}^{k(f)} \sum_{i=1}^{n_i} \frac{y_{ijm}}{l_{ijm}} .$$

At the individual plot level, averaging the k_{ij} individual estimators generates the estimator for the point-based sample unit. This estimator is model-unbiased under the assumption that the level of

CWD tallied is linearly related to the length of the transect that falls within the forested condition. The population-level estimator is generated by averaging the M cluster plot estimators.

As in the case of classifying individual plots, estimation is more complicated when the goal is to generate estimates for subpopulations. These estimates might be for a single condition class (e.g., old growth, private lands) or for pieces with specific characteristics. For example, an analyst interested in the abundance of CWD pieces that could serve as dens for Canadian lynx might be interested in knowing the total number of hollow CWD pieces in decay class 1 or 2 that are longer than 30 feet and have a large-end diameter greater than 45 inches. Both estimation problems can be addressed by treating the population as a domain of interest (Cochran 1977, Chapter 2.13) within the forest population. Some additional notation is required because a subpopulation can be related to both the condition class where the CWD piece is located (i.e., condition class c) and the characteristics of each individual piece, which will be denoted by ∂. Thus, let $\overline{Y}(c, \partial)$ denote the per acre estimator for all CWD in condition, c, that have the characteristic ∂. The estimator for the domain of interest requires the definition of the indicator variable, which takes on the value of 1 when the piece of CWD is in the subpopulation of interest and 0 otherwise.

The population-level estimator for the domain of interest is:

$$\overline{Y}(c, \partial) = \frac{1}{M} \sum_{m=1}^{M} \overline{Y}_m = \frac{1}{M} \sum_{m=1}^{M} \frac{\pi}{2 \sum_{j=1}^{k(f)} L_j(f)} \sum_{j=1}^{k(f)} \sum_{i=1}^{n_i} \frac{y_{ijm} \delta(c, \partial)}{l_{ijm}}, \quad (3.20)$$

where δ_{ijm} is 1 if CWD piece i on transect j of plot m falls on condition class c and domain ∂. Note that all transects within the population of interest (i.e., forested land) are used in the estimation. An example is given in appendix 8.2. Comparing the examples in appendices 8.1 and 8.2 illustrates the difference between estimating for classification and estimating population characteristics.

3.4 Estimation for Monitoring and in Conjunction with other FIA Inventories

DWM data can be used to monitor trends in DWM using a variety of techniques (e.g., Urquhart et al. 1998) and in conjunction with other inventories. Other components of the FIA inventory program may be used in estimation/analytical procedures with the DWM indicator. Phase 1 provides forest/nonforest stratification information necessary to produce population estimates of DWM components. Additionally, phase 1 may provide imagery required for mapping DWM estimates (e.g., fuel maps) (Woodall 2003, Woodall et al. 2004). Phase 2 inventories may be used to both provide strata for population estimates (e.g., forest type, county, and ownership class) and data for development of phase 2/phase 3 modeling efforts. If models can be developed to predict DWM components for all phase 2 plots (based on the subset of sampled phase 3 plots), then additional estimation procedures can be developed for alternative population estimates and mapping methodologies.

Because DWM sampling occurs directly on FIA inventory plots in conjunction with other phase 3 indicators, cross-indicator estimation and analysis procedures are possible and warrant future exploration (O'Neill et al. 2004, 2005). Two forest health indicators that are most likely candidates for estimation and analysis in conjunction with the DWM indicator are soils and vegetative structure and diversity. Carbon pools may be estimated conjointly between the soils and DWM inventories. The DWM indicator provides the data for CWD and FWD carbon estimation, and the soils indicator provides litter and duff carbon estimates (O'Neill et al. 2004). The vegetative structure and diversity indicator may help refine shrub/herb processing algorithms. Currently the DWM indicator does not collect species information for shrub/herb components, whereas the vegetation indicator may provide valuable constants for processing data from the DWM microplot. Analysts who undertake cross-indicator analyses and estimation procedures should be aware of any potential overlaps among indicators (e.g., soils and DWM both sample duff depths) and discrepancies in the spatial location of indicator sampling (e.g., soils indicator samples off-plot for carbon while the DWM indicator collects samples only on the FIA subplot).

3.5 DWM Data Processing

Applying any estimator to DWM data sets requires database programming; an overview and outline of the necessary database program will be provided in this section. Data processing algorithms, within the framework of the National Information Management System (NIMS), facilitate the production and management of DWM field data and subsequent core tables. A processing algorithm manipulates DWM field data such that DWM estimators may be applied and concise output tables produced at the plot, condition class, and population levels. The first step for data processing involves applying

DWM estimators at the plot level. Because estimation requires individual DWM component-, transect-, and plot-level measurements for proper application of estimation protocol, processing codes are predominated by database management routines. Hence, construction of a DWM processing program entails a rather complicated architecture of DWM data management with DWM estimators (with associated equation constants see appendix 8.5) inserted at critical junctures in the code. However, the processing code (appendix 8.4) can be loosely organized according to DWM component and the data requirements of each estimator (fig. 3.1).

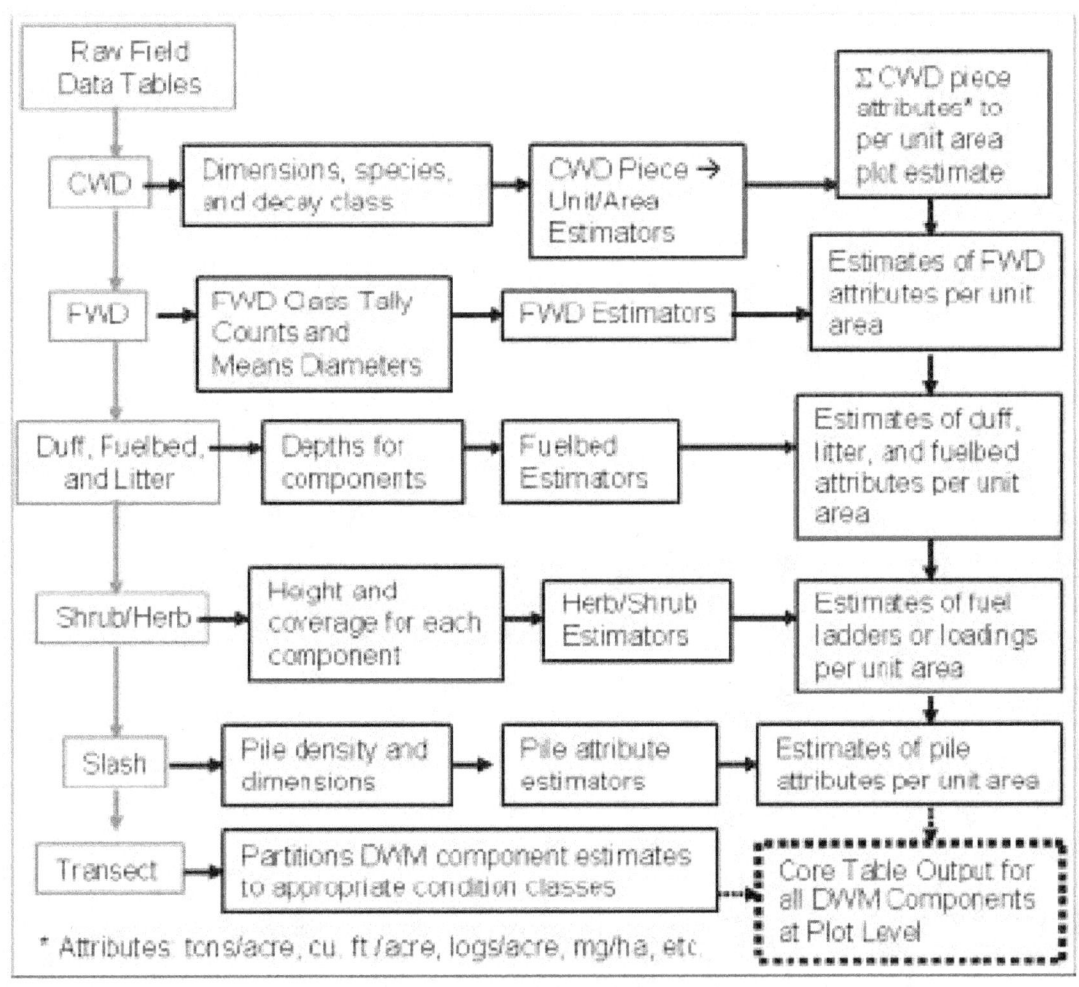

Figure 3.1.—Data processing flowchart for fire science-oriented core table.

4. CHANGE ESTIMATION

Change in DWM would be most efficiently estimated by re-measuring the same set of plots at two points in time. This cannot be accomplished on all FIA plots because a small portion of the plots will either leave or enter the population that meets FIA's definition of forest land when the plot is measured at the second visit. FIA field crews have raised an additional concern, which is that a substantial amount of damage/disturbance to both FWD and CWD can occur in the process of data collection on the plot, regardless of how careful the field crews are. This damage to the resource could cause inflated estimates of the rates of decay. One solution would be to move at least some of the data collection for DWM off of the plot and use these data to test or adjust for damage due to trampling.

Because most field crews do not permanently mark CWD or FWD pieces, it is assumed that each individual woody piece will not be relocated and measured during remeasurement activities. Unlike phase 2 standing tree protocols that track individual trees over time to assess ecosystem change, the DWM sample protocols are designed to estimate plot-level down woody attributes. Over large scales, DWM protocols and estimators are designed to indicate whether fuels, wildlife habitat, or carbon pools are significantly different. Therefore, plot-level DWM estimates may be compared over time; however, results must be couched in the underlying statistical theory and general goals of the DWM indicator. Change is most likely best estimated among large strata such as forest or stand types.

5. DWM ANALYTICAL GUIDELINES

To facilitate efficient and accurate analysis of DWM data, forest inventory analysts should be well versed in the sampling protocol, estimators, and processing of DWM field data. Beyond this knowledge of the DWM indicator, being aware of all analyses possible with DWM data can aid analysts with their task of DWM data dissemination and interpretation. Analysis of DWM data follows a hierarchy based on level of sophistication and data processing: field data, plot-summary core tables, population core tables, tabular/graphical summaries, and maps. Analysis of DWM data will also depend on access to actual data, with FIA analysts having access to actual plot locations. Data users outside of FIA may have reduced access to plot locations and less ability to link DWM data to all phases of FIA's inventory program. However, the analysis presented in this section should be widely available to all.

5.1 Field Data

Although field data provide the base of any analytical exploration of DWM, analysts will only infrequently deal with raw, field data. Field data are organized into one of six tables (tables 1.2-1.7). There is no processing of field data present in DWM data tables. Researchers engaged in specific DWM studies may use these data sets where their investigations require unique processing and/or summarization of field data. Otherwise, analysts may want to focus their resources on provided plot and population core tables and mapping efforts. Examples of processing code are provided in the appendices merely as a starting point for analysts who wish to conduct their own field data processing for specific/regional research objectives.

5.2 Plot Summary Core Tables

Plot summary core tables provide application and summarization of DWM estimators at the plot level. Core tables are currently produced for, but not limited to, three science disciplines: fire, carbon, and wildlife. These tables may serve as the basis of DWM investigations for most analysts. If analysts prefer using alternative DWM estimators or wish to add their own refinements to the DWM processing algorithms, they will need to process field data independently. There is no single way to process DWM data that allows analysts the freedom to pursue their own scientific explorations. Provided DWM core tables are simply one set of processed DWM tables that will be publicly available.

A fire science-oriented core table (table 1.8) contains estimates of fuel loadings per unit area for each DWM phase 3 plot using one set of DWM estimators. State/regional forest analysts may use a fire core table to summarize fuel loadings for delineated areas of at least a "super county" size (super county may be a conservation district that encompasses numerous counties). Holistic assessments of fire hazard may be gained by combining the fire core table with ancillary data sets such as topography, phase 2 stand information, meteorological data, and wildland-urban interface information. Carbon processing algorithms that contain estimators, constants, and data set fields desired by the carbon modeling scientific community produce carbon-oriented core tables (table 5.1). Because the soils indicator collects information on duff and litter, the DWM carbon core table is constructed to avoid data set overlap of carbon pools. Analysts may use the carbon core tables, in combination with other phases of the FIA inventory, to assess and monitor carbon pools of forest ecosystems for delineated areas. Wildlife core tables (table 5.2) are outputs from advanced data processing of CWD field data (table 1.2). Wildlife biologists want information about the quantity and quality of habitat for fauna with CWD niches. Hence, wildlife core tables contain not only volume and tonnage estimates of CWD per plot, but also size- and decay-class distributions along with species composition (table 5.2).

Table 5.1.—Processed DWM data oriented toward carbon estimation, plot level

State	County	Plot	FWD*	CWD*	Duff*	Slash*
xxx	17	385	0.7	7.2	16.7	0
xxx	31	434	2.7	3.5	22.3	0
xxx	31	436	0.9	3.7	12.1	0
xxx	31	439	1.3	5.1	17.8	0
xxx	31	442	0.2	2.2	21.0	0
xxx	31	446	3.7	0.4	7.4	4.9
xxx	31	109	3.1	1.3	2.9	0
xxx	31	120	2.5	5.5	34.2	0
xxx	31	900	1.2	2.3	15.0	0

*mg/ha

Table 5.2.—Processed DWM data oriented toward wildlife emphases, plot level

Plot	CWD (ft³/ac)	Size class* (pieces/acre)				Decay class (pieces/acre)				
		3.0-7.9	8.0-12.9	13.0-17.9	18.0-22.9	1	2	3	4	5
xxx	205.53	68	0	0	0	0	0	0	0	68
xxx	974.18	252	0	0	0	0	0	0	51	201
xxx	582.52	139	0	0	0	0	0	37	102	0
xxx	835.57	159	0	0	0	0	81	0	38	40
xxx	978.84	409	0	0	0	0	0	0	0	409
xxx	479.56	166	108	0	0	0	180	0	94	0
xxx	585.30	0	0	71	0	0	0	0	71	0
xxx	968.23	355	69	0	0	0	0	0	400	24
xxx	819.73	0	0	14	0	159	0	0	0	14

*Transect diameter (in.)

5.3 Population-Level Core Tables

Expansion of DWM plot estimates to larger area estimates (i.e., super county, State, or regional scales) produces population core tables. This type of core table is of interest to analysts seeking single estimates of DWM components for delineated areas as opposed to the distribution of plot-level values as provided by plot core tables. Estimates of carbon among CWD and forest floor components are most likely to be included in a population core table.

Although not a population estimate, per acre means of DWM components among forest type strata are recommended as core tables to be presented in required reports (tables 5.3 and 5.4). These summaries by forest type may provide fuel (table 5.3) and habitat (table 5.4) summaries by an ecologically significant stratification (i.e., forest types). For certain areas, other ecological delineations such as Bailey's (1995) ecological provinces or FIA units may be considered as summarization strata. Analysts may need to combine forest types into broader forest type groups to achieve a level of statistical significance. Finally, although not included in tables 3.4 and 3.5, standard errors of the means may be included to aid users in data evaluation.

5.4 Tabular and Graphical Summaries

DWM data summary tables may be presented by numerous methods (figs. 5.1 and 5.2). The scale

Table 5.3.—*Proposed State-level DWM core table containing means of fuel loading variables by forest type*

Forest type	1-hr	10-hr	100-hr	1,000-hr	Duff	Litter	Fuelbed depth (ft)	Shrub/ herbs (ft)
Spruce/Fir	0.1	1.1	2.0	3.9	25.0	7.6	1.1	2.2
Pine	0.2	2.0	0.2	10.1	18.6	4.4	0.8	2.9
Elm/Ash	0.8	0.4	1.9	8.7	12.9	7.3	1.7	1.4
Beech/Birch	1.1	0.9	2.2	7.8	32.0	10.1	1.2	4.0
Oak	0.0	1.2	0.9	11.1	18.0	3.4	0.9	3.3
Oak/Pine	0.7	1.3	2.9	14.0	17.5	2.9	3.0	2.1

* All estimates tons/acre except where indicated

Table 5.4.—*Proposed State-level DWM core table containing means of both carbon estimates and coarse woody debris attributes by forest type*

Forest type	FWD Carbon (Mg/ha)	CWD Carbon (Mg/ha)	CWD (ft³/ac)	Size class* (pieces/acre)				Decay class (pieces/acre)				
				3.0- 7.9	8.0- 12.9	13.0- 17.9	18.0- 22.9	1	2	3	4	5
Spruce/Fir	8.9	20.2	205.5	68	5	0	0	0	2	0	3	68
Pine	11.1	58.2	974.1	252	15	1	3	6	0	13	51	201
Elm/Ash	8.7	13.8	582.5	139	12	0	0	0	6	37	102	6
Beech/Birch	5.5	19.8	585.3	10	22	71	0	2	30	0	71	0
Oak	18.9	25.6	968.2	355	45	0	4	2	0	0	400	2
Oak/Pine	15.4	30.1	819.7	22	8	14	0	30	0	7	0	7

*Transect diameter (in.)

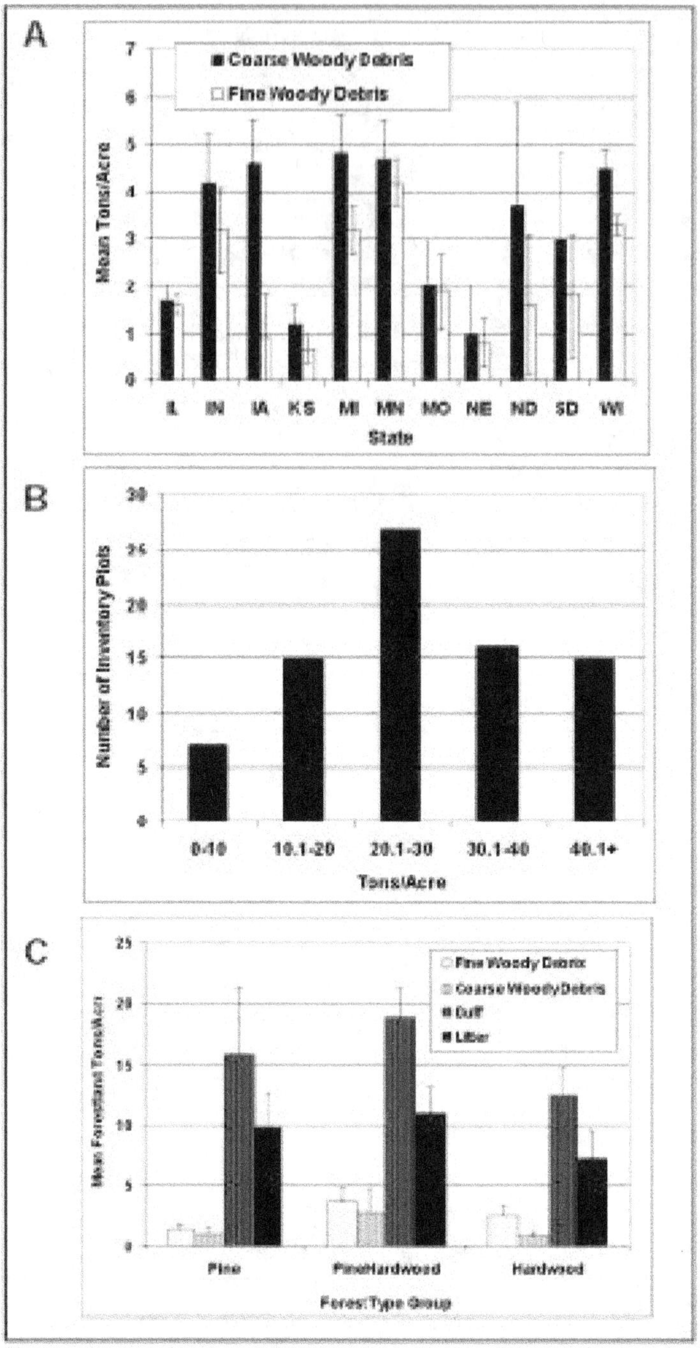

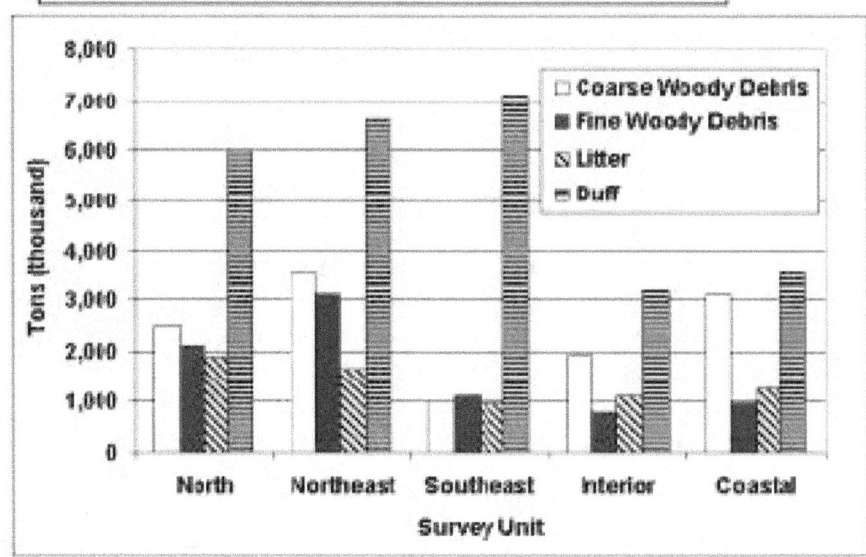

Figure 5.1.—Examples of DWM plot summaries. (A) Mean tons/acre of DWM attributes by State. (B) Distribution of sample plots according to DWM attributes in user-defined area. (C) Mean of DWM attribute by ancillary data such as forest type.

Figure 5.2.—Example of DWM population summaries, estimates of DWM attributes for a State (total tons, 1,000).

and available DWM sample size determine which DWM summaries are available to analysts. Summarizing county-scale DWM plots may not be possible, where counties at best have only one DWM sample plot. Analysts must determine the variances associated with their summaries to determine which scale is appropriate for summary. Hence, often the most logical scale for summary of DWM data is the State or super-county level at normal sample intensity (fig. 5.1a). DWM data summaries at scales smaller than a State may be permissible in States with extensive forest areas or when sample intensification occurs. The difference between plot and population summary charts is the units of summarization (figs. 5.1 and 5.2). Plot-level summarizations will often be mean per unit area values (fig. 5.1a) (i.e., mean tons/acre of CWD for DWM plots) or distribution of plot-level estimates (fig. 5.1b). Additionally summaries may occur by linking phase 2 stand information to DWM core tables providing additional data such as forest type and landowner information (fig. 5.1c). DWM plot core tables may be produced using this ancillary information to fill user requests (fig. 5.1c).

Population core table summaries will often provide estimates of an entire population of DWM components within a defined area (fig. 5.2). Defined areas will once again depend on the sample size of DWM

phase 3 plots contained within. If variances allow, analysts may produce a summary chart for super-county scales. Obvious from examples (tables 5.3, 5.4; figs. 5.1, 5.2), analysts may use DWM core tables in conjunction with the entire FIA inventory to produce summary tables and figures to satisfy numerous needs of user groups.

5.5 Maps

Maps of DWM components may be created by a number of methods requiring various data inputs and levels of sophistication (fig. 5.3). At the very least, perturbed locations of DWM phase 3 plots and associated estimates of DWM components are necessary for creating maps. Ancillary data sets that aid the DWM map creation process are ecological provinces, phase 2 data, and phase 1 forest/non-forest maps. Maps let analysts use their own creative freedom to provide new and desired outputs for users.

The first type of map is the most basic for analysts to create—a map of fuzzed plot locations and associated estimates of DWM components. An analyst may use GIS software to display fuzzed plot locations colored according to associated DWM component. Based on regional needs, these basic maps may be tailored to suit specific, regional

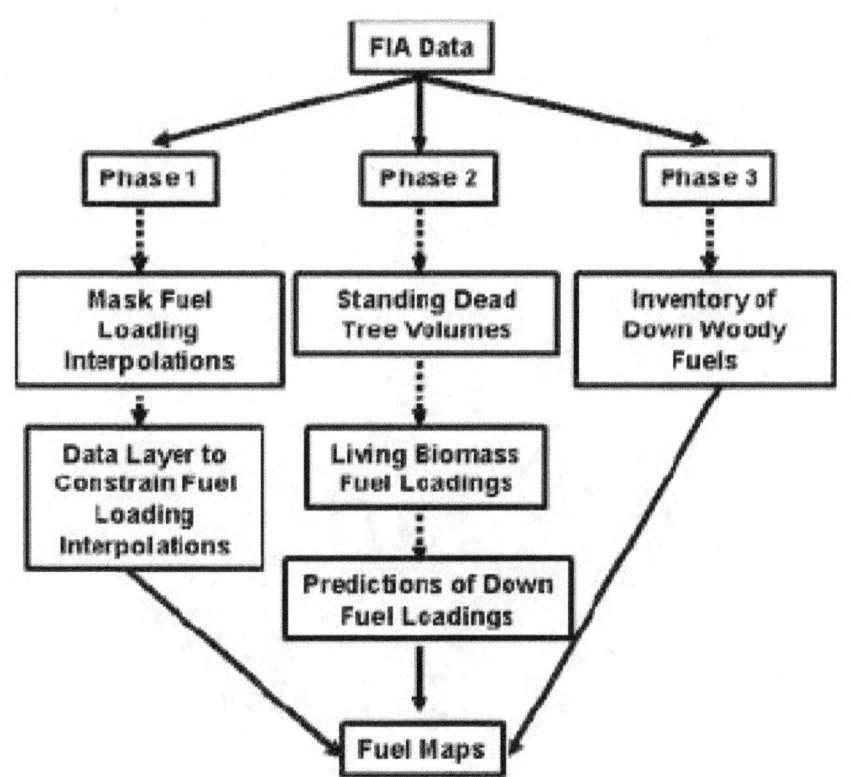

Figure 5.3.—Data contributions from all phases of the FIA inventory program provide numerous methodologies for creating national fuels maps.

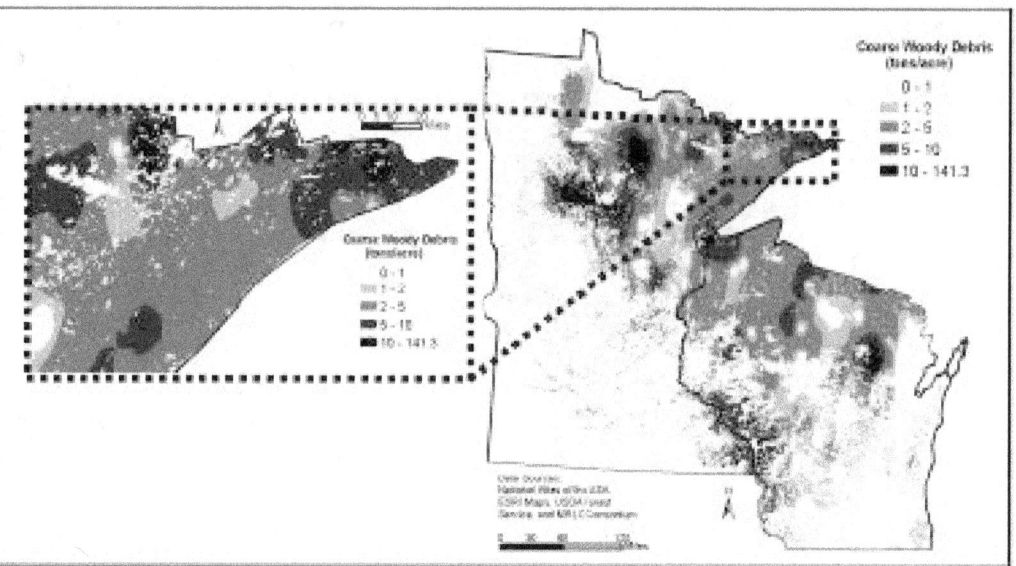

Figure 5.4.—Estimates of total tons of DWM for Boundary Waters Canoe Area, northern Minnesota, 2001 DWM inventory.

issues. As an example, increased DWM sampling intensity of DWM plots in the Boundary Waters of Minnesota may be "zoomed" in for users to gain a better idea of the distribution of fuel loadings in the scale of interest, with the rest of the DWM sampling grid providing context for these fuel loadings (fig. 5.4). Maps such as these can answer the critical question: are my local fuel loadings different from those in the rest of my region?

Ancillary data sets that are spatial in nature may also be used to create maps of DWM components (fig. 5.5). Mean values of DWM components may be estimated for any spatial data layer. Maps may be created in unison with

ecological province, forest type, or fire condition class maps (fig. 5.5).

Maps may be created using interpolation techniques (fig. 5.6). Interpolation simply involves predicting the values of DWM components between all sample points to create a continuous map of predicted DWM values (Woodall et al. 2004). DWM maps may be created one of two ways by using interpolation methodologies. First, an analyst may constrain interpolation to forested areas as defined by FIA phase 1 stratification imagery. Second, an analyst may simply overlay an interpolated map of DWM values on that of a forest nonforest map, thus masking out all nonforest areas (fig. 5.6).

Figure 5.5.—Mean estimates of total tonnage fuel loading for North Central ecological provinces based on 2001-2002 DWM inventory.

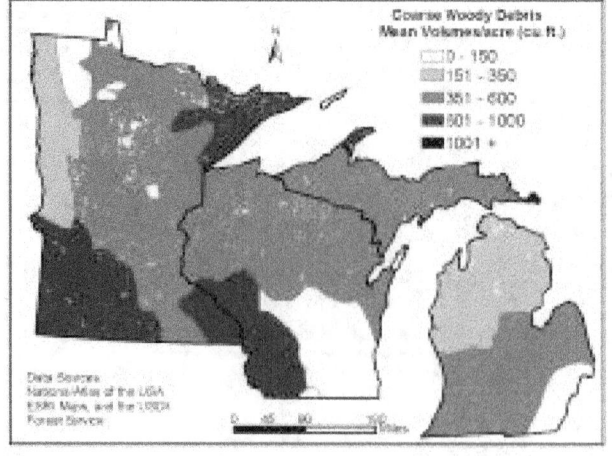

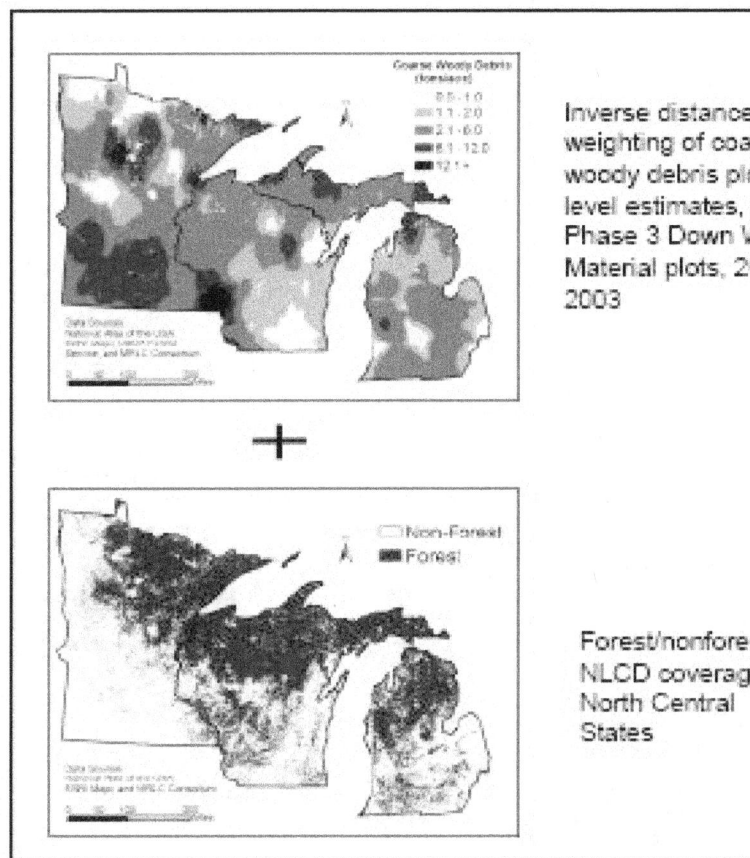

Inverse distance weighting of coarse woody debris plot-level estimates, FIA Phase 3 Down Woody Material plots, 2001-2003

Forest/nonforest NLCD coverage for North Central States

Figure 5.6.—Interpolation techniques for creating regional maps of DWM component estimates.

Maps may be created by intensive modeling efforts based on FIA phase 2 data (fig. 5.7). This process uses both phase 2 and 3 data to create models whereby DWM components are estimated for every phase 2 plot. Once satisfactory models are created, DWM components may be estimated for every phase 2 plot and mapped (fig. 5.7). Although the sampling intensity is much greater for phase 2 plots, the efficacy of this methodology depends on the explanatory power of the models established between phase 2 and 3 plots.

The mapping of DWM indicator data is a relatively recent analytical undertaking that allows maximum freedom for analysts with a few stringent guidelines. Every method for producing maps of DWM estimates has advantages and disadvantages, and it is suggested that analysts explore all their options.

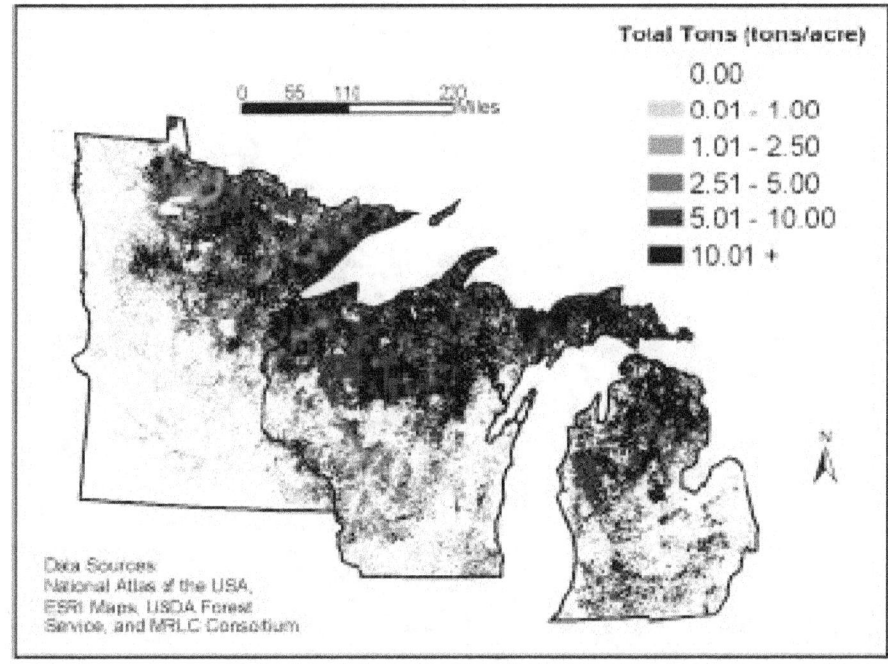

Figure 5.7.—Interpolation of predicted down fuels for FIA Phase 2 plots based on Phase 2/Phase 3 fuel models, North Central States 2001-2002 (McRoberts et al. 2004).

6. REFERENCES

Anonymous. 1995.
Sustaining the world's forests: the Santiago Declaration. Journal of Forestry. 93(4): 18-21.

Anonymous. 1997.
First approximation report on the Montreal Process. Working group on criteria and indicators for the conservation and sustainable management of temperate and boreal forest. Ottawa, Canada: The Montreal Process Liaison Office, Natural Resources Canada, Canadian Forest Service. 47 p.

Bailey, R.G. 1995.
Description of the ecoregions of the United States, 2d ed. Misc. Publ. 1391. Washington, DC: U.S. Department of Agriculture, Forest Service. 108 p.

Bebber, D.P.; Thomas, S.C. 2003.
Prism sweeps for coarse woody debris. Canadian Journal of Forest Research. 33: 1737-1743.

Bechtold, W.A.; Patterson, P.L., eds. In press.
Forest Inventory and Analysis national sample design and estimation procedures. Gen. Tech. Rep. SR-. Knoxville, TN: U.S. Department of Agriculture, Forest Service, Southern Research Station. 106 p.

Bell, G.; Kent, A.; McNickle, D.; Woolons, R. 1996.
Accuracy of the line intersect method if post-logging sampling under orientation bias. Forest Ecology and Management. 84: 23-28.

Brown, J.K. 1974.
Handbook for inventorying downed woody material. Gen. Tech. Rep. INT-16. Ogden, UT: U.S. Department of Agriculture, Forest Service, Intermountain Forest and Range Experiment Station. 24 p.

Brown, J.K.; Marsden, M.A. 1976.
Estimating fuel weights of grasses, forbs, and small woody plants. Res. Note. INT-210. Ogden, UT: U.S. Department of Agriculture, Forest Service, Intermountain Forest and Range Experiment Station. 11 p.

Brown, J.K.; Roussopoulos, P.J. 1974.
Eliminating biases in the planar intersect method for estimating volumes of small fuels. Forest Science. 20: 350-356.

Brown, J.K.; Oberhue, R.D.; et al. 1982.
Handbook for inventorying surface fuels and biomass in the interior West. Gen. Tech. Rep. INT-129. Ogden, UT: U.S. Department of Agriculture, Forest Service, Intermountain Forest and Range Experiment Station. 45 p.

Bull, E.L.; Parks, C.G.; Torgersen, T.R. 1997.
Trees and logs important to wildlife in the Interior Columbia River Basin. Gen. Tech. Rep. PNW-391. Portland, OR: U.S. Department of Agriculture, Forest Service, Pacific Northwest Research Station. 55 p.

Burgan, R.E. 1988.
1988 Revisions to the 1978 National Fire-Danger Rating System. Res. Pap. SE-273. Asheville, NC: U.S. Department of Agriculture, Forest Service, Southeastern Forest Experiment Station. 39 p.

Canfield, R.H. 1941.
Application of the line interception method in sampling range vegetation. Journal of Forestry. 39: 388-394.

Cochran, W.G. 1977.
Sampling techniques. 3d ed. New York, NY: Wiley. 448 p.

Deeming, J.E.; Burgan, R.E.; Cohen, J.D. 1977.
The National Fire-Danger Rating System - 1978. Gen. Tech. Rep. INT-39. Ogden, UT: U.S. Department of Agriculture, Forest Service, Intermountain Forest and Range Experiment Station. 63 p.

De Vries, P.G. 1973.
A general theory on line intersect sampling with application to logging residue inventory. No. 73-11. Wageningen, The Netherlands: Mededdlingen Landbouw Hoeschool. 24 p.

De Vries, P.G. 1974.
Multi-stage line intersect sampling. Forest Science. 20: 129-133.

De Vries, P.G. 1986.
Sampling theory for forest inventory: a teach-yourself course. Chapter 13: Line-intersect sampling. Berlin, Germany: Springer-Verlang: 242-279.

Ducey, M.J.; Gove, J.H.; Valentine, H.T. 2004.
A walk-through solution to the boundary overlap problem. Forest Science. 50: 427-435.

Gillespie, A.J.R. 1999.
Rationale for a national annual forest inventory program. Journal of Forestry. 97(12): 16-20.

Gove, J.H.; Ringvall, A.; Stahl, G.; Ducey, M.J. 1999.
Point relascope sampling of downed coarse woody debris. Canadian Journal of Forest Research. 29: 1718-1726.

Gregoire, T.G. 1998.
Design-based and model-based inference in survey sampling. Canadian Journal of Forest Research. 28: 1429-1447.

Gregoire, T.G.; Monkevich, N.S. 1994.
The reflection method of line-intersect sampling to eliminate boundary bias. Environmental Ecological Statistics. 1: 219-226.

Gregoire, T.G.; Valentine, H.T. 2003.
Line intersect sampling: ell-shaped transects and multiple intersections. Environmental Ecological Statistics. 10: 263-279.

Hardy, C.C. 1996.
Guidelines for estimating volume, biomass, and smoke production for piled slash. Gen. Tech. Rep. PNW-364. Portland, OR: U.S. Department of Agriculture, Forest Service, Pacific Northwest Research Station. 21 p.

Harmon, M.E.; Franklin, J.F.; Swanson, F.J.; et al. 1986.
Ecology of coarse woody debris in temperate ecosystems. Advanced Ecology Research. 15: 133-302.

Heath, L.S.; Birdsey, R.A. 1997.
A model for estimating the U.S. Forest carbon budget. In: Birdsey, R.; Mickler, R.; Sandberg, D.; et al., eds. USDA Forest Service Global Change Research Program Highlights: 1991-95. Gen. Tech. Rep. NE-237. Radnor, PA: U.S. Department of Agriculture, Forest Service, Northeastern Research Station: 107-119.

Husch, B.; Miller, C.I.; Beers, T.W. 1972.
Forest mensuration. New York, NY: Ronald. 410 p.

Kaiser, L. 1983.
Unbiased estimation in line-intersect sampling. Biometrics. 39: 965-976.

Keyes, C.; Rogers, P.; LaMadeleine, L.; et al. 2003.
Utah forest health report: a baseline assessment: 1999-2001. Salt Lake City, UT: Utah Division of Forestry, Fire and State Lands. 54 p.

Loomis, R.M. 1977.
Jack pine and aspen forest floors in northeastern Minnesota. Res. Note NC-222. St. Paul, MN: U.S. Department of Agriculture, Forest Service, North Central Forest Experiment Station. 3 p.

Lucas, H.A.; Seber, G.A.F. 1977.
Estimating coverage and particle density using the line intercept method. Biometrika. 64: 68-622.

Marshall, P.L.; Davis, G.; LeMay, V.M. 2000.
Using line intersect sampling for coarse woody debris. Tech. Rep. TR-003. Vancouver, BC: Research Section, Vancouver Forest Region, BC Ministry of Forests. 34 p.

Maser, C.; Anderson, R.G.; Cromack, K., Jr.; et al. 1979.
Dead and down woody material. In: Thomas, J.W., tech. ed. Wildlife habitats in managed forests: the Blue Mountains of Oregon and Washington. Agric. Handb. 553. Washington, DC: U.S. Department of Agriculture, Forest Service: 78-95.

McRoberts, R.E.; Williams, W.H.; Reams, G.A.; et al. 2004.
Assessing sustainability using data from the Forest Inventory and Analysis program of the United States Forest Service. Journal of Sustainable Forestry. 18: 23-46.

Nalder, I.A.; Wein, R.W.; Alexander, M.E.; deGroot, W.J. 1997.
Physical properties of dead and downed round-wood fuels in the boreal forests of Alberta and Northwest Territories. Canadian Journal of Forest Research. 27: 1513-1517.

Nalder, I.A.; Wein, R.W.; Alexander, M.E.; deGroot, W.J. 1999.
Physical properties of dead and downed round-wood fuels in the Boreal forests of western and northern Canada. International Journal of Wildland Fire. 9: 85-99.

Nemec, A.F.L.; Davis, G. 2002.
Efficiency of six line-intersect sampling designs for estimating volume and density of coarse woody debris. Tech. Rep. TR-021. Vancouver, BC: Research Section, Vancouver Forest Region, BC Ministry of Forests.

O'Neill, K.P.; C.W. Woodall, C.W.; Amacher, M.C. 2004.
Cross-indicator analysis: combining inventories of soil and down woody material to assess carbon storage at the regional scale. In: Proceedings, Society of American Foresters national conference: 2003 October 5-9: Buffalo, NY: 102-110.

O'Neill, K.; Woodall, C.W.; Holden, R.A.; Amacher, M.C. 2005.
Linking soils and down woody material inventories for cohesive national assessments of carbon. In: McRoberts, R., ed. Proceedings, Fourth annual FIA science symposium and the southern forest mensurationists: 2002 November 19-21: New Orleans, LA. Gen. Tech. Rep. NC-252. St. Paul, MN: U.S. Department of Agriculture, Forest Service, North Central Research Station: 27-32.

Pickford, S.G.; Hazard, J.W. 1978.
Simulation studies on line intersect sampling of forest residue. Forest Science. 24: 469-483.

Ringvall, A.; Stahl, G. 1999.
Field aspects of line intersect sampling for assessing coarse woody debris. Forest Ecology and Management. 119: 163-170.

Roussopoulos, P.J.; Johnson, V.J. 1973.
Estimating slash fuel loadings for several lake state tree species. Res. Pap. NC-88. St. Paul, MN: U.S. Department of Agriculture, Forest Service, North Central Forest Experiment Station. 7 p.

Schmidt, T.L.; Hansen, M.H.; Solomakos, J.A. 2000.
Indiana's forests in 1998. Resour. Bull. NC-196. St. Paul, MN: U.S. Department of Agriculture, Forest Service, North Central Research Station. 139 p.

Sollins, P. 1982.
Input and decay of coarse woody debris in coniferous stands in western Oregon and Washington. Canadian Journal of Forest Research. 12: 18-28.

Stahl, G. 1998.
Transect relascope sampling—a method of quantifying coarse woody debris. Forest Science. 44: 58-63.

Stahl, G.; Ringvall, A.; Fridman, J. 2001.
Assessment of coarse woody debris —a methodological overview. Ecology Bulletin. 49: 57-70.

Tkacz, B.M. 2002.
Forest health monitoring. Washington, DC: U.S. Department of Agriculture, Forest Service, State and Private Forestry, Forest Health Protection. [Online] Available: http://www.fs.fed.us/foresthealth/fhm/index.htm.

Urquhart, N.S.; Paulsen, S.G.; Larsen, D.P. 1998.
Monitoring for policy-relevant regional trends over time. Ecological Applications. 8: 246-257.

U.S. Department of Agriculture, Forest Service. 1999a.
A strategic plan for forest inventory and monitoring. Washington, DC: U.S. Department of Agriculture, Forest Service. 20 p.

U.S. Department of Agriculture, Forest Service. 2004.
National core field guide. Vol. II, Field data collection procedures for phase 3 plots. Section 14. Down woody materials. 33 p.

Van Wagner, C.E. 1964.
The line-intersect method in forest fuel sampling. Forest Science. 10: 267-276.

Van Wagner, C.E. 1982a.
Graphical estimation of quadratic mean diameters in the line-intersect method. Forest Science. 28: 852-855.

Van Wagner, C.E. 1982b.
Practical aspects of the line intersect method. Inform. Rep. PI-X-12. Petawawa National Forestry Institute, Canadian Forestry Service. 18 p.

Waddell, K.L. 2002.
Sampling coarse woody debris for multiple attributes in extensive resource inventories. Ecology Industries. 1: 139-153.

Warren, W.G.; Olsen, P.F. 1964.
A line-intersect technique for assessing logging waste. Forest Science. 10: 267-276.

Williams, M.S.; Eriksson, M. 2002.
Comparison of two paradigms for fixed-area sampling. Forest Ecology and Management. 168: 135-148

Williams, M.S.; Gove, J.H. 2003.
Perpendicular distance sampling: an alternative method for sampling downed coarse woody debris. Canadian Journal of Forest Research. 33: 1564-1579.

Woldendorp, G.; Keenan, R.J.; Ryan, M.F. 2002.
Coarse woody debris in Australian forest ecosystems. Canberra, ACT, Australia: Department of Agriculture, Fish and Forestry. 75 p.

Woodall, C.W. 2003.
Coming soon: a national assessment of fuel loadings. Journal of Forestry. 101(2): 4-5.

Woodall, C.W.; Holden, G.R.; Vissage, J.S. 2004.
Large scale maps of forest fuels. Fire Management Today. 64(2): 19-21.

7. GLOSSARY

Coarse Woody Debris (CWD): Down pieces of wood with a minimum small-end diameter of at least 3 inches and a length of at least 3 feet (excluding decay class 5). CWD pieces must be detached from a bole and/or not be self-supported by a root system with a lean angle more than 45 degrees from vertical.

Decay class: Rating of individual coarse woody debris according to a 5-class decay scale defined by the texture, structural integrity, and appearance of pieces. Scale ranges from freshly fallen trees to completely decomposed cubicle rot heaps.

Down Woody Materials (DWM): A term used to collectively describe attributes estimated by the Down Woody Materials indicator. A majority of the indicator's components are down and dead forest materials: fine woody debris, coarse woody debris, duff, litter, slash, live and dead herb and shrubs, and fuelbed depths.

Duff: Organic forest floor layer consisting of decomposing leaves and other organic material in which individual plant parts are not recognizable.

Fine Woody Debris (FWD): Down woody pieces with a diameter less than 3 inches at the point of transect intersection excluding dead branches attached to standing trees, dead foliage, bark fragments, or cubicle rot.

Fuelbed: Accumulated mass of all DWM components above the top of the duff layer (excluding live shrubs/herbs).

Fuel Hour Classes: Fuel classes defined by the amount of time it roughly takes for moisture conditions to fluctuate. Larger coarse woody debris will inherently take longer to dry out than smaller fine woody pieces (Small FWD=1-hour, Medium FWD=10-hour, Large FWD=100-hour, CWD=1,000-hour).

Herbs: Nonwoody herbaceous plants, but also ferns, moss, lichens, sedges, and grasses.

Integrated Fuel Depth: Estimator that scales the maximum height of all shrub/herb components based on their associated coverage. Useful for incorporating all four shrub/herb measurements into single estimate of fuel ladder heights.

Line-Intersect Sampling (LIS): Sampling technique by which sampling planes are installed in defined areas of interest whereby intersection of down woody debris with sampling planes are used to estimate coarse and fine woody populations.

Litter: Forest floor layer of freshly fallen leaves, needles, twigs, cones bark chunks, dead moss, dead lichens, dead herbaceous stems, and flower parts.

Pile Density: The density of coarse woody debris in slash piles within the volume defined by the shape code and dimensions estimated by field crews, also known as packing ratio.

Shrubs: Herbaceous plants with woody stems.

Slash: Otherwise known as residue piles, coarse woody debris in piles created directly from human activity or from natural events that prohibit safe measurement by transects.

Transect Diameter: Diameter of coarse woody pieces at the point of intersection with sampling planes.

Transect Segment: Sections of transects that lie entirely within one condition class whereby one 24-foto transect that lies across two condition classes will have two transect segments.

"Y" Transect: The spatial arrangement of sampling transects on FIA subplots whereby they radiate out from subplot center at obtuse angles of 120 degrees from each other.

8. APPENDICES

8.1 Example: Classifying Plots Based on the Level of CWD

This example will illustrate the estimation process when the goal is to classify the forested conditions found on the plot based on the level of CWD. For this discussion, assume the goal is to classify each plot into categories that correspond to arbitrarily selected low, medium, and high levels of CWD, where the low category may be defined as lands having CWD levels of < 350 ft³/acre, the medium category may be 351-600 ft³/acre, and the high category may be lands having more than 600 ft³/acre.

Figure 8.1 depicts an FIA plot that covers three different forest conditions. Subplots 1 and 2 fall completely within condition class $c = 1$, which is land that meets the definition of low levels of CWD volume. Subplot 3 straddles condition classes $c = 1$ and $c = 2$, with condition class $c = 2$ meeting the definition of high levels of CWD volume. Subplot 4 falls predominantly in condition class $c = 1$, but a small portion falls in condition class $c = 3$, which also has a high level of CWD, but for the purpose of discussion it will be a distinctly different condition class. For example, condition class 3 could be privately owned land and condition class 2 could be National Forest land.

The data for calculating the level of CWD on this plot are given in tables 1.2 and 1.5. These data must be further manipulated and combined to

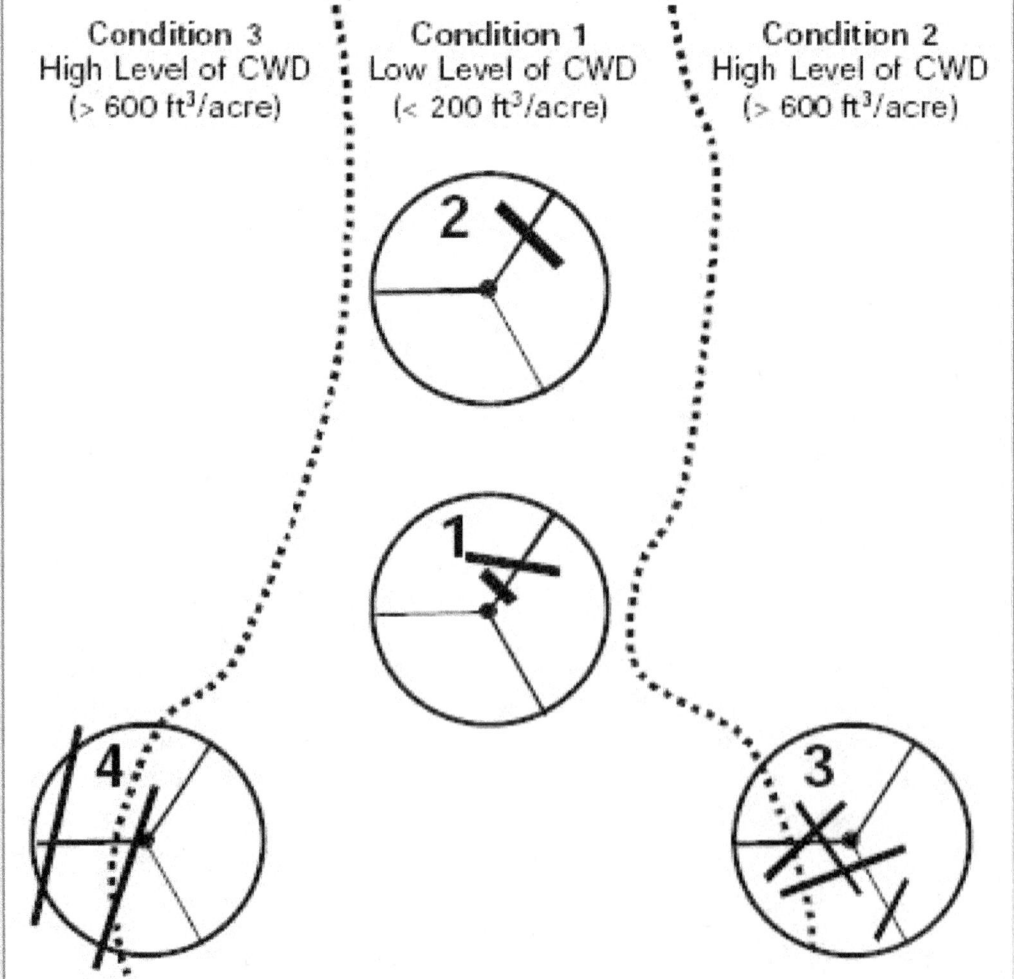

Figure 8.1.—Hypothetical plot map and corresponding condition classes for CWD estimation procedure example one, appendix 8.1.

perform the estimation. The first step is to determine the volume of each piece of CWD using equation 3.4 in conjunction with columns 7,8, and 9 in table 1.2.

V_g
0.56
10.14
4.61
1.34
17.15
4.66
1.64
85.34
8.48

The next task is to calculate the total transect length within each condition (i.e., $L(c), c = 1,2,3$) using the information in table 1.5. This yields

$$\sum_{j=1}^{k(1)} L_j(1) = 224.9, \sum_{j=1}^{k(2)} L_j(2) = 59.5,$$

and

$$\sum_{j=1}^{k(3)} L_j(3) = 3.4.$$

All that remains is to estimate the volume per acre of CWD on each condition using equation 3.10, where the per unit area conversion factor is $f = 43,560$, and the length of each piece, (l_j), is given in table 1.2. This yields cubic foot volume per acre estimates of $\bar{Y}(1) = 303.7$, $\bar{Y}(2) = 931.4$, and $\bar{Y}(3) = 30,130$.

Note that the estimate for condition class $c = 3$ greatly exceeds any reasonable level of CWD volume in the Eastern U.S. This outrageous overestimate occurs because a single piece of CWD is tallied on a very short section of transect ($\sum_{j=1}^{k(3)} L_j(3)$ = 3.4). This result should not be surprising given that the literature clearly states (e.g., Marshall et al. 2000, Nemac and Davis 2002, Pickford and Hazard 1978) that total transect lengths of close to 1,000 meters are required to achieve a high level of precision with LIS estimators. Thus, whenever the total transect length in condition class c is small (i.e., $\sum_{j=1}^{k(c)} L_j(c) \leq 24$ ft or one transect length at a minimum), the resulting estimate is likely to incorrectly classify the condition. Such results should not be used in any analysis because the sampling effort (i.e., the length of transect) is far too short to produce reliable information.

8.2 Example: Estimation of Population Totals for CWD

This example will illustrate the estimation process when the goal is to estimate the population total for CWD as well as the total for one of the condition classes. As illustrated in appendix 8.1, it is possible to generate unrealistic estimates for individual condition class when classifying the level of CWD in each condition class.

The data used in this example include the FIA plot data used in the appendix 8.1 and one additional plot; these plots are illustrated in figure 8.2 and will be referred to as plot 1 and plot 2, respectively.

The first task is calculating the volume for each piece of CWD, which gives

V_g	V_g
plot 1	plot 2
0.56	53.78
10.14	31.02
4.61	2.13
1.34	0.99
17.15	8.96
4.66	10.83
1.64	8.2
85.34	8.2
8.48	10.12

The next task is to calculate the total transect length that falls within the population, which is the total length of transects that fall on land that meets FIA's definition of forest. Using the data in table 1.5 yields

$$\sum_{j=1}^{k(f)} L_j(f) = 288, \sum_{j=1}^{k(f)} L_j(f) = 237.9,$$

for plots 1 and 2, respectively.

All that remains is to estimate the volume per acre of CWD for the population using equation 3.11, where the per unit area conversion factor is $f = 43,560$, and the length of each piece, (l_j), is given in table 1.2. This yields cubic foot volume per acre estimates of plot 1 and 2 of $\bar{Y}_1 = 785.8$, $\bar{Y}_2 = 1,218.0$, and the overall population estimate of $\bar{Y} = 1/2(785.8 + 1,218.0) = 1,001.9$ ft³/acre.

Estimating the attributes for either condition classes or domains requires the defining the indicator

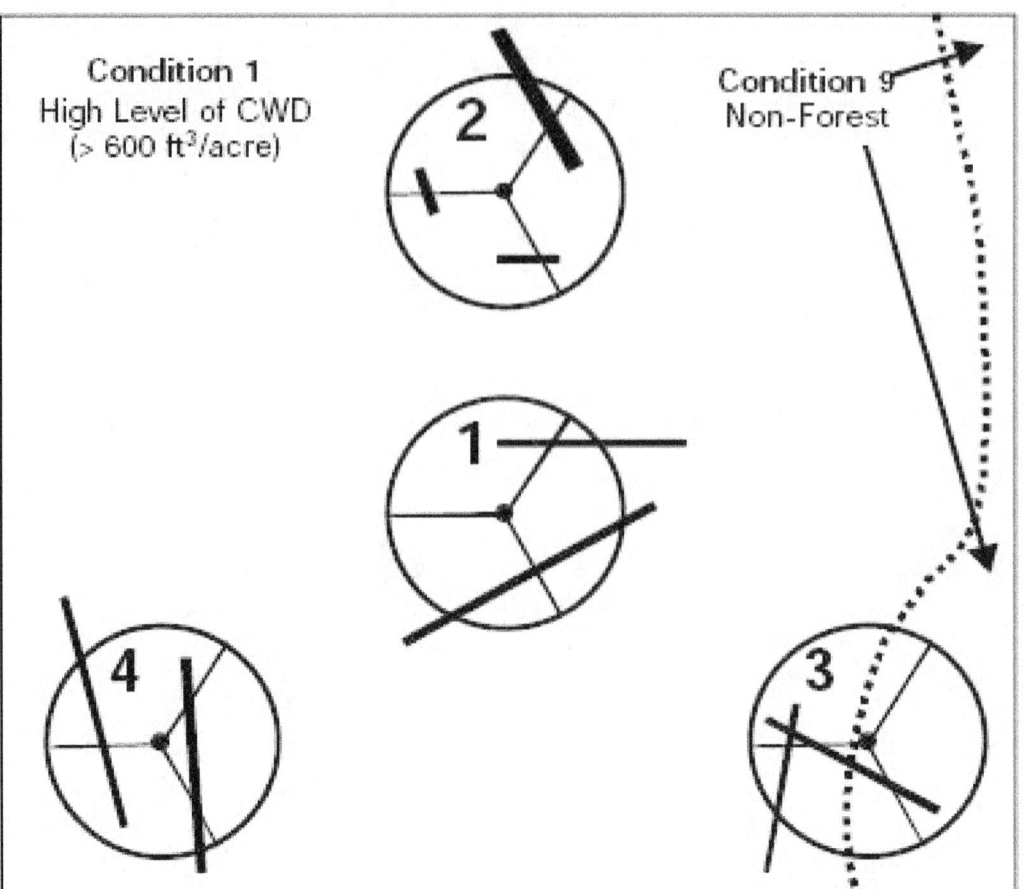

Figure 8.2.—Hypothetical plot map and corresponding condition classes for CWD estimation procedure example two, appendix 8.2.

variable $\delta(c,\partial)$ that takes on the value of 1 when a piece of CWD is tallied on condition class c and meets the definition of domain ∂. To illustrate, assume that the goal is to generate an estimate of the volume of CWD in condition class $c = 2$ for all logs in decay classes 1, 2, or 3. From table 1.2, it can be discerned that $\delta(c = 2, \partial) = (0,0,0,1,1,0,1,0,0,0,0,0,0,0,0,0,0,0)$. Using equation 3.13 yields $\overline{Y}(c,\partial) = 76.5$ ft³/acre.

8.3 Example: Estimation of Mean Fuel Loadings by Forest Type for Large Area

The citizens of the state of "C" would like estimates of their fuels for common forest types of their forests. They are not interested in who owns these forests or where the fuels are exactly located. Rather, they would like a broad estimate of where they stand when it comes to risks of wildfire. State "C" has only 28 DWM plots established over a full cycle of inventory. The estimates of fuel loadings for these plots are provided either by the national DWM indicator advisor, regional FIA staff, or a national data distribution web site. Next, the analyst must link the unique identifier of each DWM plot with corresponding phase 2 inventory data to summarize fuel estimates by forest type or any other forest condition attribute. An important note is that one DWM plot may contain more than one forested condition, thus there may be numerous forest types for one DWM plot. If fuel estimates were determined at the condition class level, then they may be easily averaged. However, plot estimates may be available only at the plot level. In this instance the condition proportion of each forest type may be used to weight the mean of the fuel loadings determined for each forest type. An example of such PL-SQL code is provided in appendix 8.4. Once mean and standard errors estimates of fuels by forest types are determined for state "C" (table 8.3.1), analysts must determine how to display the results. With only 28 DWM plots sampled in state "C," certain forest types have only 1 plot while others have only 2 or 3 (table 8.3.1). We suggest that means for strata, such as forest type, be presented only if more than a few

Table 8.3.1.—*Initial fuel loading estimates by forest type for hypothetical state "C" presented in appendix section 8.3*

Forest type group	#Plots	1-hr	10-hr	100-hr	1,000-hr	Duff	Litter	Shrubs/Herbs*
White/Red/Jack pine	2	1.04	2.88	1.69	1.58	7.47	5.05	0.38
Oak/Pine	1	0.97	3.04	1.20	0.32	4.27	1.76	1.17
Oak/Hickory	17	0.38	1.05	1.49	3.74	5.56	2.19	1.23
Elm/Ash/Cottonwood	3	0.13	0.34	1.92	24.31	2.35	0.51	3.10
Maple/Beech/Birch	4	0.36	0.56	1.37	44.25	2.03	10.26	0.37
Aspen/Birch	1	0.33	2.43	1.81	4.48	2.63	3.16	0.10

*feet

plots have been sampled in said strata. Because forest conditions are so varied across the United States, analysts will have to rely on interpretation of standard errors to determine the appropriate sample size for including means in any inventory reports. For state "C", the pine forest types may be combined into the conifer forest type group with 3 plots, the oak/hickory forest type group may remain the same with 17 plots, while the remaining forest types may be combined into an "other hardwoods" forest type group with 8 plots (table 8.3.1). Analysts should couch decisions on how to present fuel estimates, which often have a low sample size, in the ecological significance of a forest type group and the variance associated with mean estimates.

8.4 DWM PROCESSING CONSTANTS

Species number	Genus	Species	Specific gravity	Slash bulk density (lbs/ft³)	Fine woody debris (dia²)			Litter bulk density (lbs/ft³)	Duff bulk density (lbs/ft³)
					Small (in.)	Medium (in.)	Large (in.)		
10	Abies	spp.	0.34	21.20					
11	Abies	amabilis	0.40	25.00					
12	Abies	balsamea	0.34	21.20	0.005	0.194	2.402	1.1	7.2
14	Abies	bracteata	0.36	22.50					
15	Abies	concolor	0.37	23.10	0.013	0.205	1.792	4.9	11.4
16	Abies	fraseri	0.34	21.20					
17	Abies	grandis	0.35	21.80	0.0122	0.304	2.87	5.07	11.07
19	Abies	lasiocarpa	0.31	19.30	0.0122	0.304	3.12	5.07	11.07
20	Abies	magnifica	0.36	22.50	0.016	0.205	2.517	7.5	11.4
21	Abies	magnifica var. shastensis	0.36	22.50					
22	Abies	procera	0.37	23.10					
41	Chamaecyparis	lawsoniana	0.39	24.30					
42	Chamaecyparis	nootkatensis	0.42	26.20					
43	Chamaecyparis	thyoides	0.31	19.30					
50	Cupressus	spp.	0.44	27.50					
60	Juniperus	spp.	0.44	27.50					
64	Juniperus	occidentalis	0.44	27.50	0.012	0.25	2.157	4.4	11.1
69	Juniperus	monosperma	0.45	28.10					
70	Larix	spp.	0.44	27.50					
71	Larix	laricina	0.49	30.60	0.041	0.169	2.82	1	2
72	Larix	lyallii	0.48	30.00					
73	Larix	occidentalis	0.48	30.00	0.0151	0.238	2.17	5.07	11.07
81	Calocedrus	decurrens	0.37	23.10					
90	Picea	spp.	0.38	23.70					
91	Picea	abies	0.38	23.70					
92	Picea	breweriana	0.33	20.60					
93	Picea	engelmannii	0.33	20.60	0.0122	0.304	2.87	5.07	11.07
94	Picea	glauca	0.37	23.10	0.006	0.24	2.91	1.1	7.2
95	Picea	mariana	0.38	23.70	0.006	0.24	2.91	1.1	7.2
96	Picea	pungens	0.38	23.70					
97	Picea	rubens	0.38	23.70					
98	Picea	sitchensis	0.37	23.10					
101	Pinus	albicaulis	0.37	23.10	0.02	0.188	2.286	3.7	11
102	Pinus	aristata	0.37	23.10					
103	Pinus	attenuata	0.37	23.10	0.016	0.194	1.499	2.4	13.7
104	Pinus	balfouriana	0.37	23.10	0.018	0.143	1.987	5.6	13.1
105	Pinus	banksiana	0.40	25.00	0.021	0.266	3.207	1.1	7.2
106	Pinus	edulis	0.50	31.20					
107	Pinus	clausa	0.46	28.70					
108	Pinus	contorta	0.38	23.70	0.0201	0.344	2.87	5.89	10.15
109	Pinus	coulteri	0.37	23.10					
110	Pinus	echinata	0.47	29.30					
111	Pinus	elliotti	0.54	33.70					
112	Pinus	engelmannii	0.37	23.10					

Species number	Genus	Species	Specific gravity	Slash bulk density (lbs/ft³)	Fine woody debris (dia²)			Litter bulk density (lbs/ft³)	Duff bulk density (lbs/ft³)
					Small (in.)	Medium (in.)	Large (in.)		
113	Pinus	flexilis	0.37	23.10	0.024	0.194	2.682	6.2	14
114	Pinus	strobiformis	0.35	21.80					
115	Pinus	glabra	0.41	25.60					
116	Pinus	jeffreyi	0.37	23.10	0.033	0.198	2.747	2	10.5
117	Pinus	lambertiana	0.34	21.20	0.019	0.227	2.11	2.5	10
118	Pinus	leiophylla	0.37	23.10					
119	Pinus	monticola	0.35	21.80	0.014	0.219	1.792	3.1	8.7
120	Pinus	muricata	0.37	23.10					
121	Pinus	palustris	0.54	33.70					
122	Pinus	ponderosa	0.38	23.70	0.0342	0.238	3.12	2.25	9.67
123	Pinus	pungens	0.49	30.60					
124	Pinus	radiata	0.37	23.10					
125	Pinus	resinosa	0.41	25.60	0.031	0.242	2.518	2.5	4.3
126	Pinus	rigida	0.47	29.30					
127	Pinus	sabiniana	0.37	23.10	0.021	0.146	2.009	2.1	8.1
128	Pinus	serotina	0.51	31.80					
129	Pinus	strobus	0.34	21.20	0.012	0.176	2.56	1.1	7.2
130	Pinus	sylvestris	0.41	25.60					
131	Pinus	taeda	0.47	29.30					
132	Pinus	virginiana	0.45	28.10					
133	Pinus	monophylla	0.50	31.20					
133	Pinus	nigra	0.41	25.60					
134	Pinus	discolor	0.50	31.20					
135	Pinus	arizonica	0.37	23.10					
202	Pseudotsuga	menziesii	0.45	28.10	0.0122	0.304	2.87	6.33	9.52
211	Sequoia	sempervirens	0.34	21.20					
212	Sequoiadendron	giganteum	0.34	21.20	0.021	0.198	2.644	8.8	10.1
221	Taxodium	distichum var. nutans	0.42	26.20					
231	Taxus	brevifolia	0.60	37.40					
241	Thuja	occidentalis	0.29	18.10	0.066	0.221	2.19	5.07	11.07
242	Thuja	plicata	0.31	19.30	0.0122	0.304	2.87	5.07	11.07
251	Torreya	californica	0.34	21.20					
260	Tsuga	spp.	0.38	23.70					
263	Tsuga	heterophylla	0.42	26.20	0.007	0.226	2.11	7.2	11.5
264	Tsuga	mertensiana	0.42	26.20	0.007	0.226	2.11	7.2	11.5
299		softwood	0.38	23.70					
300	Acacia	spp.	0.60	37.40					
310	Acer	spp.	0.49	30.60					
311	Acer	barbatum	0.54	33.70					
312	Acer	macrophyllum	0.44	27.50					
313	Acer	negundo	0.44	27.50					
314	Acer	nigrum	0.52	32.40					
315	Acer	pensylvanicum	0.44	27.50					
316	Acer	rubrum	0.49	30.60	0.028	0.159	2.517	0.9	6
317	Acer	saccharinum	0.44	27.50					
318	Acer	saccharum	0.56	34.90					

Species number	Genus	Species	Specific gravity	Slash bulk density (lbs/ft³)	Fine woody debris (dia²)			Litter bulk density (lbs/ft³)	Duff bulk density (lbs/ft³)
					Small (in.)	Medium (in.)	Large (in.)		
319	Acer	spicatum	0.44	27.50					
321	Acer	glabrum	0.44	27.50					
322	Acer	grandidentatum	0.44	27.50					
330	Aesculus	californica	0.38	23.70					
330	Aesculus	spp.	0.33	20.60					
341	Ailanthus	altissima	0.37	23.10					
350	Alnus	spp.	0.37	23.10					
355	Amelanchier	spp.	0.66	41.20					
361	Arbutus	menziesii	0.58	36.20					
367	Asimina	triloba	0.47	29.30					
370	Betula	spp.	0.48	30.00					
371	Betula	alleghaniensis	0.55	34.30					
372	Betula	lenta	0.60	37.40					
373	Betula	nigra	0.56	34.90					
374	Betula	occidentalis	0.53	33.10					
375	Betula	papyrifera	0.48	30.00	0.016	0.167	2.89	0.9	6
376	Betula	papyrifera var. commutata	0.48	30.00					
379	Betula	populifolia	0.45	28.10					
381	Bumelia	lanuginosa	0.47	29.30					
391	Carpinus	caroliniana	0.58	36.20					
400	Carya	spp.	0.62	38.70					
401	Carya	aquatica	0.61	38.10					
402	Carya	cordiformis	0.60	37.40					
403	Carya	glabra	0.66	41.20					
404	Carya	illinoensis	0.60	37.40					
405	Carya	laciniosa	0.62	38.70					
406	Carya	myristicaeformis	0.56	34.90					
407	Carya	ovata	0.64	39.90					
408	Carya	texana	0.54	33.70					
409	Carya	tomentosa	0.64	39.90					
421	Castanea	dentata	0.40	25.00					
422	Castanea	pumila	0.40	25.00					
423	Castanea	ozarkensis	0.40	25.00					
430	Castanopsis	spp.	0.42	26.20					
450	Catalpa	spp.	0.38	23.70					
460	Celtis	spp.	0.49	30.60					
461	Celtis	laevigata	0.47	29.30					
462	Celtis	occidentalis	0.49	30.60					
471	Cercis	canadensis	0.58	36.20					
475	Cercocarpus	ledifolius	1.00	62.40					
476	Cercocarpus	montanus	1.00	62.40					
479	Cercocarpus	intricatus	1.00	62.40					
481	Cladrastis	lutea	0.52	32.40					
490	Cornus	spp.	0.64	39.90					
491	Cornus	florida	0.64	39.90					
492	Cornus	nuttallii	0.58	36.20					

Species number	Genus	Species	Specific gravity	Slash bulk density (lbs/ft³)	Fine woody debris (dia²)			Litter bulk density (lbs/ft³)	Duff bulk density (lbs/ft³)
					Small (in.)	Medium (in.)	Large (in.)		
500	Crataegus	spp.	0.62	38.70					
510	Eucalyptus	spp.	0.67	41.80					
521	Diospyros	virginiana	0.64	39.90					
531	Fagus	grandifolia	0.56	34.90					
540	Fraxinus	spp.	0.54	33.70					
541	Fraxinus	americana	0.55	34.30					
542	Fraxinus	latifolia	0.50	31.20					
543	Fraxinus	nigra	0.45	28.10					
544	Fraxinus	pennsylvanica	0.53	33.10					
545	Fraxinus	profunda	0.54	33.70					
546	Fraxinus	quadrangulata	0.53	33.10					
551	Gleditsia	aquatica	0.60	37.40					
552	Gleditsia	triacanthos	0.60	37.40					
555	Gordonia	lasianthus	0.37	23.10					
571	Gymnocladus	dioicus	0.50	31.20					
580	Halesia	spp.	0.32	20.00					
591	Ilex	opaca	0.50	31.20					
600	Juglans	spp.	0.51	31.80					
601	Juglans	cinerea	0.36	22.50					
602	Julglans	nigra	0.51	31.80					
611	Liquidambar	styraciflua	0.46	28.70					
621	Liriodendron	tulipifera	0.40	25.00					
631	Lithocarpus	densiflorus	0.58	36.20					
641	Maclura	pomifera	0.76	47.40					
650	Magnolia	spp.	0.45	28.10					
660	Malus	spp.	0.61	38.10					
680	Morus	spp.	0.59	36.80					
681	Morus	alba	0.59	36.80					
682	Morus	rubra	0.59	36.80					
691	Nyssa	aquatica	0.46	28.70					
692	Nyssa	ogeche	0.46	28.70					
693	Nyssa	sylvatica	0.46	28.70					
701	Ostrya	virginiana	0.63	39.30					
711	Oxydendrum	arboreum	0.50	31.20					
712	Paulownia	tomentosa	0.38	23.70					
721	Persea	borbonia	0.51	31.80					
731	Platanus	occidentalis	0.46	28.70					
740	Populus	spp.	0.37	23.10					
741	Populus	balsamifera	0.31	19.30	0.022	0.258	2.89	0.9	6
742	Populus	deltoides	0.37	23.10					
743	Populus	grandidentata	0.36	22.50	0.022	0.258	2.89	0.9	6
744	Populus	heterophylla	0.37	23.10					
745	Populus	deltoides	0.37	23.10					
745	Populus	sargentii	0.37	23.10					
746	Populus	tremuloides	0.35	21.80	0.022	0.258	2.89	0.9	6
747	Populus	balsamifera	0.31	19.30					
748	Populus	fremontii	0.34	21.20					

43

Species number	Genus	Species	Specific gravity	Slash bulk density (lbs/ft³)	Fine woody debris (dia²)			Litter bulk density (lbs/ft³)	Duff bulk density (lbs/ft³)
					Small (in.)	Medium (in.)	Large (in.)		
749	*Populus*	*angustifolia*	0.34	21.20					
752	*Populus*	*alba*	0.37	23.10					
755	*Prosopis*	spp.	0.58	36.20					
760	*Prunus*	spp.	0.47	29.30					
761	*Prunus*	*pensylvanica*	0.36	22.50					
762	*Prunus*	*serotina*	0.47	29.30					
763	*Prunus*	*virginiana*	0.36	22.50					
765	*Prunus*	*nigra*	0.47	29.30					
766	*Prunus*	*americana*	0.47	29.30					
800	*Quercus*	spp.	0.58	36.20					
801	*Quercus*	*agrifolia*	0.70	43.70					
802	*Quercus*	*alba*	0.60	37.40					
803	*Quercus*	*arizonica, grisea*	0.70	43.70					
804	*Quercus*	*bicolor*	0.64	39.90					
805	*Quercus*	*chrysolepis*	0.70	43.70					
806	*Quercus*	*coccinea*	0.60	37.40					
807	*Quercus*	*douglasii*	0.51	31.80					
808	*Quercus*	*durandii*	0.60	37.40					
809	*Quercus*	*ellipsoidalis*	0.56	34.90					
810	*Quercus*	*emoryi*	0.70	43.70					
811	*Quercus*	*engelmannii*	0.70	43.70					
812	*Quercus*	*falcata* var. *falcata*	0.52	32.40					
813	*Quercus*	*falcata* var. *pagodaefolia*	0.61	38.10					
814	*Quercus*	*gambelii*	0.64	39.90					
815	*Quercus*	*garryana*	0.64	39.90					
816	*Quercus*	*ilicifolia*	0.56	34.90					
817	*Quercus*	*imbricaria*	0.56	34.90					
818	*Quercus*	*kelloggii*	0.51	31.80					
819	*Quercus*	*laevis*	0.52	32.40					
820	*Quercus*	*laurifolia*	0.56	34.90					
821	*Quercus*	*lobata*	0.64	39.90					
822	*Quercus*	*lyrata*	0.57	35.60					
823	*Quercus*	*macrocarpa*	0.58	36.20	0.028	0.1	2.82	0.9	6
824	*Quercus*	*marilandica*	0.56	34.90					
825	*Quercus*	*michauxii*	0.60	37.40					
826	*Quercus*	*muehlenbergii*	0.60	37.40					
827	*Quercus*	*nigra*	0.56	34.90					
828	*Quercus*	*nuttalli*	0.56	34.90					
829	*Quercus*	*oblongifolia*	0.70	43.70					
830	*Quercus*	*palustris*	0.58	36.20					
831	*Quercus*	*phellos*	0.56	34.90					
832	*Quercus*	*prinus*	0.57	35.60					
833	*Quercus*	*rubra*	0.56	34.90	0.028	0.1	2.82	0.9	6
834	*Quercus*	*shumardii*	0.56	34.90					
835	*Quercus*	*stellata*	0.60	37.40					

Species number	Genus	Species	Specific gravity	Slash bulk density (lbs/ft³)	Fine woody debris (dia²)			Litter bulk density (lbs/ft³)	Duff bulk density (lbs/ft³)
					Small (in.)	Medium (in.)	Large (in.)		
837	Quercus	velutina	0.56	34.90					
838	Quercus	virginiana	0.80	49.90					
839	Quercus	wislizeni	0.70	43.70					
840	Quercus	incana	0.56	34.90					
843	Quercus	hypoleucoides	0.70	43.70					
901	Robinia	pseudoacacia	0.66	41.20					
902	Robinia	neomexicana	0.66	41.20					
920	Salix	spp.	0.36	22.50					
925	Sapium	sebiferum	0.47	29.30					
931	Sassafras	albidum	0.42	26.20					
935	Sorbus	americana	0.42	26.20					
945	Tamarix	spp.	0.40	25.00					
950	Tilia	spp.	0.32	20.00					
951	Tilia	americana	0.32	20.00	0.028	0.1	2.82	5.07	11.07
952	Tilia	heterophylla	0.32	20.00					
970	Ulmus	spp.	0.50	31.20					
971	Ulmus	alata	0.57	35.60					
972	Ulmus	americana	0.46	28.70					
973	Ulmus	crassifolia	0.57	35.60					
974	Ulmus	pumila	0.46	28.70					
975	Ulmus	rubra	0.48	30.00					
976	Ulmus	serotina	0.57	35.60					
977	Ulmus	thomasii	0.57	35.60					
980	Aleurites	fordii	0.47	29.30					
981	Umbellularia	californica	0.51	31.80					
981	Vaccinium	arboreum	0.47	29.30					
983	Melia	azedarach	0.47	29.30					
984	Planera	aquatica	0.53	33.10					
985	Cotinus	obovaus	0.47	29.30					
990	Olneya	tesota	1.00	62.40					
998		hardwood	0.51	31.80					
999		unknown	0.46	28.70					

Constants may be used only as a guide for initial data analysis/processing. Citations: Brown et al. 1982; Loomis 1977; Naider et al. 1997, 1999; Roussopoulos and Johnson 1973; USDA 1999.

Because of the lack of required constant information for application of numerous DWM estimators, users may want to use the species compositions of each DWM plot to derive their own plot-specific constants. This may be done by averaging the slash bulk density, FWD diameters, litter bulk density, and duff bulk density for each species of each CWD piece identified on the CWD transects. The result would be a list of DWM estimation constants based on the unique species composition of every plot.

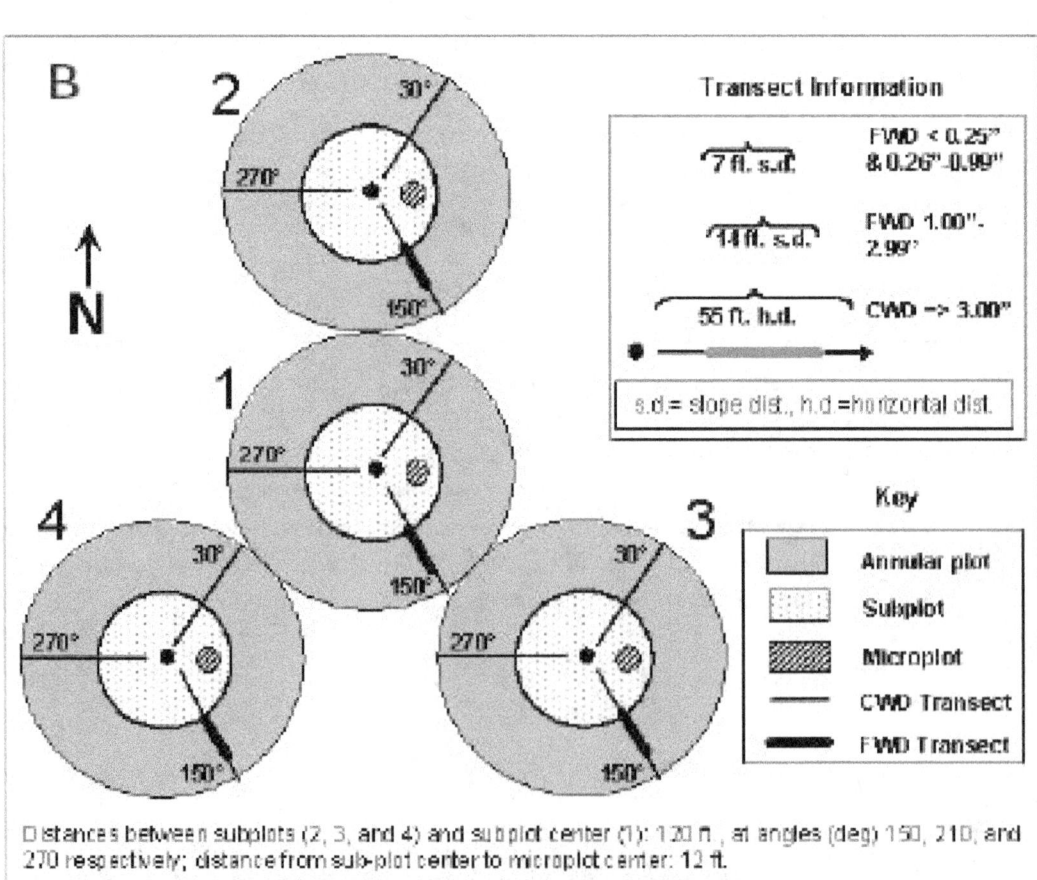

Figure 8.3.—Historic sample designs for the Forest Health Monitoring and FIA DWM programs: 1999 (A), 2000 (B), and 2001 (C).

C

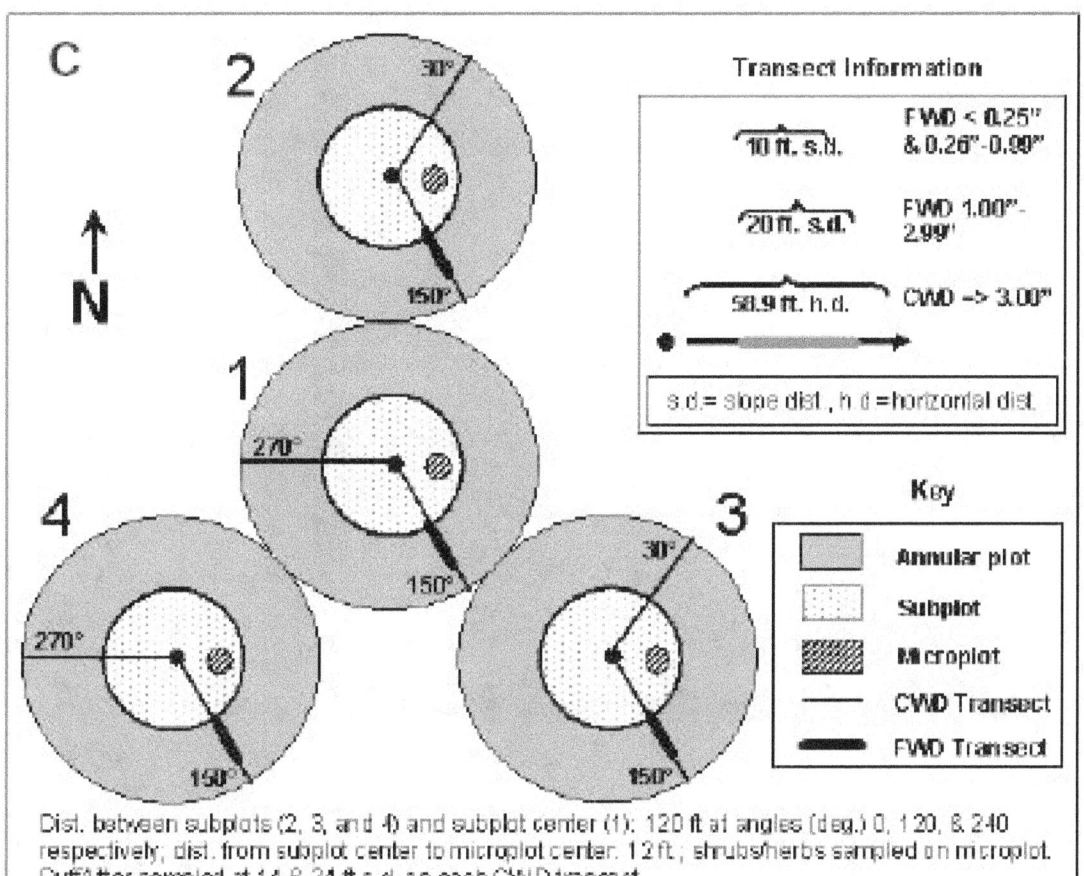

Transect Information

FWD < 0.25"
& 0.26"-0.99"
10 ft. s.d.

FWD 1.00"-
2.99"
20 ft. s.d.

CWD -> 3.00"
58.9 ft. h.d.

s.d.= slope dist., h.d =horizontal dist.

Key

Annular plot

Subplot

Microplot

CWD Transect

FWD Transect

Dist. between subplots (2, 3, and 4) and subplot center (1): 120 ft at angles (deg.) 0, 120, & 240 respectively; dist. from subplot center to microplot center: 12 ft.; shrubs/herbs sampled on microplot. Duff/litter sampled at 14 & 24 ft s.d. on each CWD transect.

Woodall, Christopher; Williams, Michael.
2005. Sampling protocol, estimation, and analysis procedures for the down woody
materials indicator of the FIA program. Gen. Tech. Rep. NC-256. St. Paul, MN: U.S.
Department of Agriculture, Forest Service, North Central Research Station. 47 p.

Provides the rationale and context for a national inventory of down woody material.
Documents the various woody material components sampled by the DWM indicator, the
sampling protocol used to measure the DWM components, and estimation procedures.
Provides guidance on managing and processing DWM data and incorporating that data
into pertinent inventory analyses and research projects.

KEY WORDS: forest inventory, down woody materials, estimation, analysis, sampling.